Cloud Empires

The Rise and Revolution of Software as a Service

Revised, September 2025

Dr Alex Bugeja, PhD

Table of Contents

- **Introduction**

- **Chapter 1**: The Genesis of the Cloud: From ASP to SaaS

- **Chapter 2**: Salesforce: The Pioneer and the Blueprint

- **Chapter 3**: The Architectural Revolution: Multi-Tenancy and Scalability

- **Chapter 4**: The Subscription Economy: A New Business Paradigm

- **Chapter 5**: The Rise of the Tech Giants: AWS, Azure, and Google Cloud

- **Chapter 6**: The API Economy: Building Interconnected Ecosystems

- **Chapter 7**: Data as the New Gold: Analytics, AI, and Machine Learning in SaaS

- **Chapter 8**: Security and Trust in the Cloud: Building Digital Fortresses

- **Chapter 9**: The User Experience (UX) Imperative: Design-Centric SaaS

- **Chapter 10**: Vertical SaaS: Conquering Niche Industries

- **Chapter 11**: The Network Effect: How Cloud Platforms Create Moats

- **Chapter 12**: Collaboration and Communication: The New Work OS

- **Chapter 13**: The Low-Code/No-Code Movement: Democratizing Software Creation

- **Chapter 14**: Navigating the Regulatory Landscape: Compliance in a Global Cloud

- **Chapter 15**: The Venture Capital Fuel: Funding the Cloud Empires

- **Chapter 16**: The Go-To-Market Playbook: Marketing and Selling SaaS

- **Chapter 17**: Customer Success: The Key to Retention and Growth

- **Chapter 18**: The Culture of Innovation: Building and Scaling SaaS Teams

- **Chapter 19**: Global Domination: The International Expansion of SaaS

- **Chapter 20**: The Dark Side of the Cloud: Vendor Lock-In and Data Privacy Concerns

- **Chapter 21**: The Serverless Future: The Evolution of Cloud Infrastructure

- **Chapter 22**: The Edge Computing Frontier: Decentralizing the Cloud

- **Chapter 23**: The Impact of AI on the Future of Software

- **Chapter 24**: Web3 and the Decentralized Application Wave

- **Chapter 25**: The Next Generation of Cloud Empires: Predicting the Future

Introduction

It is an empire built on invisibility. You don't see it, touch it, or store it in your office, yet it powers nearly every facet of modern life and global commerce. From the messages you send, to the movies you stream, to the intricate financial systems that underpin the world economy, it runs silently and ceaselessly in the background. This is the empire of the cloud, and its currency is not hardware, but access; not ownership, but subscription. Its governing philosophy is a concept that has become one of the most significant business and technological revolutions of our time: Software as a Service, or SaaS.

This book is the story of that revolution. It traces the rise of the cloud empires not just as a technological shift, but as a fundamental reimagining of how we create, distribute, and consume software. The worldwide market for SaaS was valued at over $273 billion in 2023 and is projected to grow to over a trillion dollars by 2032. This financial scale only hints at its pervasive influence. By 2025, it's expected that 85% of all business applications will be SaaS-based. Software, in essence, has evaporated from physical discs and local servers to become a utility, as accessible and ever-present as electricity from a power grid.

To understand the magnitude of this change, one must first recall the world that existed before the cloud. It was a world of on-premise software, a cumbersome and expensive reality for businesses of all sizes. Acquiring a new piece of enterprise software was a monumental undertaking, involving hefty upfront licensing fees for every user, significant investments in powerful server hardware to run it, and teams of IT specialists to perform the complex, multi-day installations. Updates were a dreaded event, often requiring manual installation across hundreds or thousands of computers, leading to downtime and compatibility nightmares.

The physical infrastructure itself was a constant burden. Companies maintained vast, air-conditioned server rooms, consuming enormous amounts of power and physical space. Managing this hardware was a full-time job for IT departments, diverting their focus from strategic innovation to mundane maintenance and troubleshooting. For smaller businesses, the cost and complexity were often insurmountable barriers, locking them out of the powerful tools that larger corporations used to dominate their industries. The software was siloed, data was difficult to access remotely, and the entire model was predicated on a cycle of expensive, infrequent upgrades.

Then, quietly at first, the revolution began. The concept wasn't entirely new; it had roots in the time-sharing systems of the 1960s and the Application Service Providers (ASPs) of the late 1990s. But these early attempts were hampered by slow, unreliable internet connections and a business model that hadn't quite ironed out the kinks. The real turning point came with the maturation of the internet and a shift in thinking, most famously championed by Salesforce in 1999, which built its customer relationship management (CRM) tool from the ground up to be delivered entirely online.

The proposition of SaaS was deceptively simple: instead of buying and installing software, you could rent it. You paid a predictable monthly or annual subscription fee, and in return, the software was always up to date, accessible from any device with an internet connection, and managed entirely by the provider. The cumbersome server rooms, the complex installations, and the costly maintenance suddenly vanished, replaced by a login screen in a web browser. This wasn't merely an evolution; it was a complete paradigm shift that would democratize technology on an unprecedented scale.

Suddenly, a small startup could access the same sophisticated software for sales, marketing, and finance as a Fortune 500 company, paying only for the "seats" it needed. This leveled the playing field, fueling a new wave of innovation and entrepreneurship. Companies could now scale their operations with incredible agility, adding or removing users as needed without the friction of procuring new hardware or licenses. The business model itself transformed capital expenditures into predictable operational expenses, freeing up cash for companies to invest in their core products and services.

This book will journey through the key milestones and innovations that built this new world. We will begin with the genesis of the idea, exploring the transition from the early ASP models to the true multi-tenant SaaS architecture that allowed for massive scalability. We will dedicate a chapter to the story of Salesforce, the company that not only pioneered the model but also wrote the playbook for how to market, sell, and grow a SaaS empire. Its success provided a blueprint that thousands of companies would follow.

We will then delve into the core technological and business principles that define the cloud empires. We'll explore the architectural revolution of multi-tenancy, the economic engine of the subscription model, and the rise of the three titans of infrastructure—Amazon Web Services (AWS), Microsoft Azure, and Google Cloud—who created the foundational platforms upon which countless SaaS businesses are built. Their story is a crucial part of this ecosystem, providing the raw computing power, storage, and networking that make the entire SaaS model viable.

The narrative will then expand to the broader ecosystem that grew around this core. We'll examine the API economy, which allowed different SaaS products to "talk" to each other, creating powerful, interconnected workflows. We will investigate how data became the new currency in this cloud-based world, fueling advancements in analytics, artificial intelligence, and machine learning that are now embedded in the software we use daily. This data-driven approach has transformed everything from customer service, which now uses AI-powered chatbots, to product design, which adapts based on user behavior.

Of course, building an empire requires more than just technology. It requires trust. We will address the critical issues of security and compliance, exploring how SaaS providers build digital fortresses to protect their customers' most sensitive information in a shared environment. We'll also look at the relentless focus on user experience (UX), a necessary evolution from the clunky, unintuitive enterprise software of the past to the sleek, consumer-grade interfaces that are now the standard.

The book will also explore the specialization and maturation of the SaaS market. We'll see how "vertical SaaS" has emerged to create tailored solutions for specific niche industries, from construction and agriculture to healthcare and finance. We'll analyze the powerful network effects that create deep moats around the most successful cloud platforms, making them incredibly difficult to displace once they reach a critical mass of users.

No revolution is without its complexities and consequences. Later chapters will navigate the ever-shifting regulatory landscapes that cloud companies must contend with, the venture capital fuel that powered their explosive growth, and the unique go-to-market strategies required to sell a subscription instead of a product. We will also turn a critical eye to the dark side of the cloud, examining pressing issues like vendor lock-in and the persistent privacy concerns that come with entrusting our data to a handful of global corporations.

Finally, we will look to the horizon, exploring the future of software itself. We will discuss the rise of serverless computing, the frontier of edge computing, and the profound impact that artificial intelligence and Web3 are poised to have on the next generation of applications. What will the cloud empires of tomorrow look like? Who will be the new titans, and what new revolutions will they unleash?

This is not just a book about technology. It is a book about a fundamental shift in business and society, driven by a simple yet powerful idea: that the most powerful tools should be accessible to everyone, anywhere, at any time. It's the story of how software escaped its physical confines to become an invisible, ubiquitous force that has reshaped our world, creating new empires in the cloud that influence every aspect of our lives.

CHAPTER ONE: The Genesis of the Cloud: From ASP to SaaS

The idea that software could be delivered as a utility, piped into businesses and homes like water or electricity, was not born in the dot-com boom of the late 1990s. Its conceptual roots reach much deeper, back to an era of room-sized mainframe computers, clattering teletype terminals, and the visionary thinking of computer science pioneers. To truly understand the revolution of Software as a Service, one must first appreciate its ancestry, a lineage of ideas that stretches back more than half a century. The cloud, in essence, is the culmination of a long-held dream: to make immense computing power accessible to many, without the burden of owning the complex machinery behind it.

This dream first took a practical form in the 1960s with the advent of "time-sharing" systems. Before this innovation, computers were monolithic beasts that could only execute one task at a time in a process known as batch processing. A programmer would submit a job, typically on a stack of punch cards, and wait—often for hours or even days—for the machine to process it and deliver the results. The computer was a scarce and astronomically expensive resource, and this inefficiency was a source of immense frustration. It was a world of delayed gratification, where a single typo in a program could mean another full day's wait to get the corrected output.

The breakthrough came from innovators like John McCarthy, who popularized the concept while at MIT. Time-sharing ingeniously allowed a single mainframe to serve multiple users simultaneously. The computer's central processing unit, or CPU, would rapidly switch between each user's tasks, dedicating a tiny "slice" of time to each one in quick succession. Because the computer operated on a timescale of microseconds, this switching was imperceptible to the human users connected via remote terminals, giving each of them the illusion that they had the machine's undivided attention. It was a clever trick of resource management that fundamentally changed the nature of human-computer interaction.

One of the first widely used systems to demonstrate this potential was the Compatible Time-Sharing System (CTSS), which went live at MIT in 1963 on a modified IBM mainframe. Suddenly, dozens of researchers could work interactively with the same computer at once, a radical departure from the solitary, one-at-a-time world of batch processing. This led to the creation of commercial time-sharing services, offered by companies like General Electric, which allowed businesses to rent computing power by the hour. These services introduced a novel billing model, charging customers for CPU seconds, storage space, and connection time, an early precursor to the usage-based pricing models common in cloud computing today.

This era of centralized computing, however, was destined for a dramatic reversal. The rise of the microprocessor in the 1970s and the subsequent personal computer (PC) revolution of the 1980s heralded a powerful new paradigm: decentralization. Companies like Apple and IBM, along with Microsoft's operating systems, put computing power directly onto the desks of individuals. The pendulum swung hard away from the shared mainframe and toward personal autonomy. This shift was driven by the falling cost of hardware; it was becoming more economical for a business to own a fleet of individual computers than to rent time on a remote behemoth.

The PC era cemented the on-premise software model. Software was a product, sold in a box. A business would buy a license for an application like Lotus 1-2-3 or WordPerfect, receive a set of floppy disks or a CD-ROM, and install it on a local computer or a server tucked away in an office closet. This model put the entire burden of ownership on the customer. They were responsible for purchasing and maintaining the server hardware, performing the installation, managing security patches, and handling the dreaded, and often costly, software upgrades. The software industry flourished under this model, but it created significant barriers for smaller companies and immense complexity for larger ones.

For the dream of centralized computing to be reborn, a critical piece of global infrastructure was needed: the internet. The popularization of the World Wide Web in the mid-1990s provided the ubiquitous, low-cost network that had been missing. It also provided a universal client in the form of the web browser. For the first time, it was technically feasible to deliver sophisticated applications to a global audience without needing to install any specialized software on their local machines. The stage was set for the next attempt to turn software into a service.

This new wave of centrally hosted software was championed by companies known as Application Service Providers, or ASPs, which emerged in the late 1990s. The value proposition of the ASP model was nearly identical to that of modern SaaS: instead of buying, installing, and managing software yourself, you could outsource it. An ASP would host a business application—for example, a customer relationship management (CRM) or an enterprise resource planning (ERP) system—in its own data center and provide access to customers over the internet for a monthly fee. This promised to reduce upfront costs, offload the IT burden, and provide access to powerful tools that might otherwise be out of reach.

Pioneering companies like USinternetworking (USi), Corio, and Interpath entered the market, generating significant buzz and attracting venture capital. They primarily targeted mid-sized companies that were struggling to manage increasingly complex software environments but lacked large IT departments. The ASPs would typically license software from established vendors like PeopleSoft, Siebel Systems, or SAP and then manage the hosting, maintenance, and support on behalf of their customers. It seemed like a win-win: software vendors could reach a new market segment, and customers could get the benefits of enterprise-grade software without the headaches.

However, the ASP model was built on a fundamentally flawed foundation. The crucial, and ultimately fatal, weakness was its architectural approach. Most ASPs operated on a single-tenant model. This meant that for each new customer, the ASP had to set

11

up a separate, dedicated instance of the application, often running on its own dedicated server. It was the on-premise model, just relocated to a different building. This approach completely undermined the economies of scale that a true service model requires. It was incredibly expensive and labor-intensive to provision, manage, and update hundreds of separate software instances.

Furthermore, the software itself was not designed for this type of delivery. The applications being hosted by ASPs were, for the most part, traditional client-server applications built with the assumption that they would be running on a company's private, high-speed local area network (LAN). When accessed remotely over the often-sluggish and unreliable internet connections of the late 1990s, these applications were painfully slow and clunky. The user experience was frequently abysmal, plagued by latency and frustratingly long load times. The software was a square peg being hammered into the round hole of the internet.

Customization and integration, two critical requirements for most businesses, were also major challenges. Since each customer had their own isolated instance, any customization had to be done on a one-off basis, a costly and time-consuming process that negated many of the model's promised benefits. Integrating the hosted application with a customer's other in-house systems was an even bigger nightmare, often requiring complex and fragile workarounds. The ASP model was brittle, inefficient, and failed to deliver on its core promise of simplicity.

The final nail in the coffin for most of the first-wave ASPs was the bursting of the dot-com bubble in 2000 and 2001. As venture capital funding dried up and the economy soured, the shaky economics of the single-tenant model became unsustainable. Many ASPs burned through their cash and went out of business, taking their customers' data and trust with them. The market had spoken, and the verdict was that while the idea was promising, the execution was deeply flawed. The term ASP became associated with failure, a cautionary tale of a good idea that was ahead of its time and, more importantly, built on the wrong technology.

Yet, even as the ASP market was collapsing, a new and far more robust model was quietly taking shape. A handful of forward-thinking companies recognized the flaws of the ASPs and were building something fundamentally different. Companies like Concur, which began its life selling packaged software on floppy disks, transitioned its travel and expense management tools to a web-based model in 2001. Another early pioneer was Intacct (now Sage Intacct), founded in 1999 with the specific goal of creating a financial accounting application designed from the ground up to be delivered via the cloud.

These companies, and the one that would soon become the standard-bearer for the new movement, understood that for the service model to work, two things had to change. First, the application architecture had to be completely rethought. Instead of the costly single-tenant model, the software had to be built on a multi-tenant architecture. This meant a single, unified instance of the application could serve all customers simultaneously, with their data securely partitioned. This was the key to achieving massive economies of scale and making the business model economically viable.

Second, the software itself had to be a true web-native application. It couldn't be a desktop application retrofitted for the web; it had to be designed from its very core to be delivered through a browser. This meant focusing on performance, usability, and a user experience that felt fast and intuitive, even over a standard internet connection. The application had to live and breathe the web. The failure of the ASPs provided a clear and valuable lesson: you couldn't simply take old-world software and put it online. You had to start over, with a new architecture and a new philosophy. This was the genesis of true Software as a Service.

CHAPTER TWO: Salesforce: The Pioneer and the Blueprint

Every revolution needs a revolutionary, and for Software as a Service, that figure was Marc Benioff. A towering presence both physically and in reputation, Benioff was a product of the very software empire he would later seek to overthrow. He had spent thirteen years at Oracle, a company that perfected the art of on-premise software sales. A protégé of its combative and legendary co-founder, Larry Ellison, Benioff had been a star, rising to become Oracle's youngest-ever vice president at the age of 26. He was a master of the old model, steeped in the world of massive upfront licensing deals, complex installations, and lucrative maintenance contracts.

Yet, despite his success, a sense of disillusionment grew. Benioff saw the deep-seated flaws in the enterprise software industry: its exorbitant costs, its frustrating complexity, and its glacial pace of innovation. He envisioned a different future, one where powerful business software could be accessed online as easily as buying a book on Amazon. This idea crystallized during a sabbatical in 1999, where he swam with dolphins in Hawaii and reflected on a new kind of company—one that delivered software over the internet and was deeply integrated with philanthropy from its very foundation. He was ready to leave his high-paying job at Oracle and take the plunge.

Returning to San Francisco, Benioff recruited three co-founders to bring his vision to life: Parker Harris, Dave Moellenhoff, and Frank Dominguez. Harris, in particular, would become the technical genius behind the throne, the architect who would solve the complex puzzle of building a true, web-native application. In March 1999, the four set up shop in a cramped one-bedroom apartment on Telegraph Hill, the closet doubling as a server room. Their mission was audacious and simple: to create a customer relationship management (CRM) service delivered entirely online, killing the old model of software distribution.

To signal their revolutionary intent, they adopted a powerful and provocative marketing mantra: "No Software." This simple, two-word slogan became their battle cry. It was a direct assault on the entire established order, a brilliant piece of branding that immediately set them apart from the incumbents like Siebel Systems, the undisputed king of CRM at the time. The "No Software" logo, a red circle with a line slashed through the word "SOFTWARE," was emblazoned on all their marketing materials, a constant reminder of their disruptive mission.

Their marketing tactics were as unconventional as their technology. They were masters of guerrilla marketing, staging audacious publicity stunts to grab headlines. In 2000, they hired actors to stage a fake protest outside a Siebel user conference, chanting anti-software slogans and carrying picket signs. For their own launch event, they rented a theater and transformed the lower level into a representation of "Enterprise Software Hell," complete with actors in cages screaming for help and games like whack-a-mole featuring the logos of their competitors. Guests had to walk through this chaotic depiction of the old world to ascend to "heaven," where the simple, clean Salesforce product was showcased.

This flair for the dramatic was essential because, in the beginning, gaining trust was their single biggest challenge. The idea of entrusting a company's most valuable asset—its customer list—to a startup's servers was, for most businesses, a terrifying proposition. The cloud was an unproven concept, and the spectacular failure of the first-wave Application Service Providers had left a trail of skepticism and burnt customers. Salesforce had to convince the world that their data would be secure, the service would be reliable, and that they, as a company, would still be around next year.

The dot-com crash of 2000, which began shortly after their founding, made this challenge even more acute. As venture capital evaporated and internet companies folded by the dozen, Salesforce was forced to navigate a brutal economic landscape. They survived through a combination of fiscal discipline, laying off 20% of their workforce to conserve cash, and an unwavering focus on their core product. The downturn, in a strange way, may have even helped them. Their subscription model, with its low, predictable monthly payments, became far more attractive to cash-strapped companies than the million-dollar upfront license fees demanded by Siebel and Oracle.

The product itself was a revelation in its simplicity. While Siebel's on-premise CRM was notoriously complex, requiring months of implementation and dedicated IT staff, the first version of Salesforce was a straightforward Sales Force Automation (SFA) tool. It was designed to be intuitive, helping salespeople track leads, manage contacts, and forecast sales, all through a web browser. The user interface was clean and easy to navigate, a stark contrast to the clunky, feature-bloated software common at the time. This focus on user experience was a critical differentiator.

Beneath this simple interface, however, was a profound technical innovation that truly set Salesforce apart from the failed ASPs of the 1990s. Parker Harris and his team had built the platform on a multi-tenant architecture. This was the secret sauce. Instead of creating a separate, costly instance of the software for each customer, multi-tenancy allowed a single, shared instance of the application to serve thousands of customers securely and efficiently. Think of it like an apartment building: all residents share the same foundational infrastructure, plumbing, and electricity, but each has their own private, secure unit.

This architecture was the key to unlocking massive economies of scale. It meant that maintaining and updating the software was radically simplified; the development team only had to update one codebase, and the improvements were instantly available to every single customer. Each customer's data was kept logically separate and secure within a shared database, identified by a unique ID. This efficiency made the low-cost subscription model economically viable, allowing Salesforce to offer enterprise-grade power at a fraction of the cost of its on-premise rivals.

The business model was just as revolutionary as the technology. When Salesforce first launched, it offered a refreshingly simple pricing plan: around $50 per user, per month. This transformed a massive capital expenditure into a predictable operational expense. Suddenly, sophisticated CRM tools were no longer the exclusive domain of Fortune 500 companies. Small and medium-sized businesses could access the same functionality, paying only for the number of users they needed and scaling up or down as required. This democratization of software leveled the playing field and unleashed a wave of productivity.

From its earliest days, Salesforce was also designed to be a different kind of company in its ethos. Benioff, inspired by his sabbatical, hardwired philanthropy into the company's operating system from day one. He created the "1-1-1 model," committing 1% of the company's equity, 1% of its product, and 1% of its employees' time to charitable causes. This integrated approach to philanthropy was a radical concept in the profit-driven world of Silicon Valley and became a core part of the company's identity, helping to attract and retain employees who were motivated by more than just stock options.

As Salesforce grew and its customer base expanded, it cultivated a vibrant and loyal community. This was epitomized by the creation of Dreamforce in 2003. What began as a relatively small user conference with just over 1,000 attendees at a San Francisco hotel would morph into one of the largest and most extravagant tech events in the world. Dreamforce became more than just a conference; it was a festival-like gathering that blended learning, networking, entertainment, and philanthropy, turning customers into evangelists and cementing Salesforce's position at the center of the cloud ecosystem.

Perhaps the most significant evolution in the company's strategy came in 2005 with the launch of the AppExchange. Benioff, reportedly taking advice from Apple's Steve Jobs, realized that Salesforce could become more than just a product; it could become a platform. The AppExchange was an online marketplace that allowed third-party developers to build and sell their own applications that ran on the Salesforce platform. This was a stroke of genius that transformed the company and the industry.

The AppExchange unlocked a torrent of innovation. Suddenly, the functionality of Salesforce could be extended in thousands of ways, tailored to specific industries and business needs, without Salesforce having to write a single line of code. If a customer needed a specialized tool for project management, accounting, or human resources that integrated with their CRM data, there was likely an app for it on the AppExchange. This created a powerful network effect: more customers attracted more developers, who built more apps, which in turn made the platform more valuable and attracted even more customers.

With this move, Salesforce created the blueprint for what it meant to be a cloud platform, a model that countless other SaaS companies would follow. They had successfully navigated the journey from a single, disruptive application to a sprawling ecosystem. They had proven that a company could deliver enterprise-grade software through a web browser, build a sustainable business on a subscription model, and create a powerful moat around their business by transforming it into a platform. Their audacity, their marketing savvy, their technological innovation, and their unique corporate culture had not only ensured their own survival and dominance but had also paved the way for the thousands of cloud empires that would rise in their wake.

CHAPTER THREE: The Architectural Revolution: Multi-Tenancy and Scalability

To the casual observer, the failure of the Application Service Providers and the subsequent triumph of Salesforce might have seemed like a simple matter of timing and marketing. The ASPs were too early, their internet connections too slow, their marketing too muddled. Salesforce, with its brilliant "No Software" campaign, simply came along when the world was ready. But this view misses the most crucial point, the seismic shift that happened below the surface. The revolution was not just in the business model; it was in the digital blueprint of the software itself. The fatal flaw of the ASPs was that they put old-world software in a new-world data center. The SaaS pioneers built something entirely new, centered on a concept that would become the engine of the cloud: multi-tenancy.

The architectural difference between the old ASP model and the new SaaS model can be understood through a simple real estate analogy. The single-tenant architecture used by most ASPs was like building a separate, single-family house for every new customer. Each house had its own foundation, its own plumbing, its own electrical wiring, and its own roof. If you wanted to upgrade the windows on every house in the neighborhood, you would have to send a crew to each individual home to do the work. This approach is private and isolated, but it is also monstrously inefficient, expensive, and difficult to manage at scale.

Multi-tenancy, in contrast, is like building a modern apartment building. A single, massive foundation and structural frame supports the entire complex. All tenants share the same core infrastructure: the main water lines, the central heating system, the elevators, and the security staff in the lobby. However, within this shared framework, each tenant has their own private, secure apartment, with its own front door and its own key. The landlord can upgrade the entire building's water heating system in one go, benefiting every resident simultaneously without having to enter each private apartment. This is the essence of multi-tenancy: a single, shared instance of an application serving multiple tenants (customers) in a way that is both highly efficient and securely partitioned.

This approach immediately solves the core economic problem that plagued the ASPs. Instead of dedicating an entire server and a separate software installation to a customer who might only have five employees, a multi-tenant provider could house that five-person company alongside a fifty-person company and a five-thousand-person company on the same shared infrastructure. The cost of the underlying hardware, the electricity to run it, and the staff to maintain it is distributed across all the tenants. This creates tremendous economies of scale, dramatically lowering the cost to serve each individual customer and making the low, predictable subscription fees of the SaaS model economically sustainable.

Of course, the idea of sharing a system with other companies, including potential competitors, raised immediate and perfectly valid concerns. The single most important challenge for any multi-tenant architect is ensuring absolute, ironclad data security and isolation. A breach where one tenant could see another's data wouldn't just be a bug; it would be an extinction-level event for the SaaS provider. The solution was to weave the concept of the tenant directly into the fabric of the application's data structure.

The pioneers of this model, like Salesforce's Parker Harris, solved this by creating a unique identifier for each customer, often called an "Organization ID" or "Tenant ID." This ID was then attached to every single piece of data that belonged to that customer. A contact, a sales opportunity, a support ticket—every row in the vast, shared database was tagged with the digital equivalent of an apartment number. When a user from a specific company logged in, the application's code was written in such a way that every query it made to the database included a crucial, non-negotiable clause: WHERE OrganizationID = '123'. This simple but ruthlessly enforced rule ensured that the application would only ever retrieve and display the data belonging to that specific tenant.

The system was designed from the ground up to be physically co-mingled but logically segregated.

The second major challenge was the "noisy neighbor" problem. In any shared environment, there is a risk that one tenant will consume a disproportionate amount of resources, slowing down the system for everyone else. One customer might run a massive, complex report, or initiate a bulk data import that monopolizes the server's processing power and database connections. This would be the digital equivalent of a neighbor in the apartment building blasting music at 3 a.m. and shaking the walls for everyone else. For a mission-critical business application, this kind of unpredictable performance is unacceptable.

To solve this, SaaS platforms instituted a system of governors and limits. These are automated controls built deep into the application's core that monitor each tenant's resource consumption in real time. The system tracks metrics like the number of API calls made in a 24-hour period, the duration of database queries, and the amount of data being processed. If a tenant exceeds these pre-defined limits, the system will gently throttle their requests or temporarily halt the offending process, preventing them from degrading the service for the wider community. While sometimes a source of frustration for developers pushing the platform's boundaries, these governors are the essential traffic cops that ensure the smooth and fair operation of the entire multi-tenant highway.

Perhaps the most elegant and complex innovation of the multi-tenant architecture, however, was the way it handled customization. A core requirement for any business software is the ability to tailor it to specific processes. A pharmaceutical sales team tracks different information than a team selling industrial machinery. The old single-tenant model handled this clumsily; to customize an application for one customer, you had to alter that customer's specific copy of the code, creating a unique version that was then difficult to upgrade. Multi-tenancy, with its single shared codebase, made this approach impossible.

The solution was a metadata-driven architecture. Instead of changing the core application code, all customizations—new data fields, modified page layouts, unique business rules, and approval processes—were defined as metadata. This metadata is essentially data that describes the application's structure and behavior for a specific tenant. When a user logs in, the application does two things: it loads the core, universal application code, and it loads that specific tenant's metadata. It then uses the metadata as a set of instructions to render the application, dynamically generating the user interface and enforcing the business logic that the customer has defined.

This was a stroke of genius. It meant that every customer could have a highly personalized version of the application while still running on the exact same core codebase as every other customer. Salesforce could push out an update with three new features, and those features would instantly become available to every single customer. The update wouldn't break any of a customer's personal customizations because those were stored separately as metadata. This provided the best of both worlds: the efficiency and rapid innovation of a shared platform, combined with the flexibility and bespoke feel of a custom-built application.

These architectural pillars—a shared infrastructure, secure data partitioning via tenant IDs, performance governors, and a metadata-driven model for customization—collectively enabled the holy grail of cloud computing: massive scalability. Scalability is the ability of a system to handle a growing amount of work by adding resources. In the context of a SaaS business, it means being able to grow from ten customers to ten thousand, and then to ten million, without a degradation in performance and without having to fundamentally re-engineer the entire platform.

There are two primary ways to scale a system. The first, known as vertical scaling or "scaling up," involves making a single server more powerful by adding more CPUs, more memory, or faster storage. This is like replacing the engine in your car with a bigger one. It's effective up to a point, but it's expensive and eventually hits a physical limit; you can only cram so much hardware into a single box. The second method is horizontal scaling, or "scaling out." This involves adding more servers to a pool of resources. This is like adding more cars to your fleet rather than just upgrading one engine.

Multi-tenant architecture is uniquely suited to horizontal scaling. Because the application is designed to be a single, stateless service shared by many, the provider can simply add more identical web and application servers to a cluster as demand grows. A device called a load balancer sits in front of this cluster, intelligently directing incoming user traffic to whichever server has available capacity. This model is incredibly flexible, resilient, and cost-effective. If a server fails, the load balancer simply stops sending traffic to it, and users are seamlessly routed to other healthy servers. If traffic surges during peak business hours, new servers can be automatically provisioned and added to the pool to handle the load, then decommissioned when demand subsides. This elastic, scale-out capability is the technical foundation that allows a company like Netflix to serve millions of simultaneous video streams or a platform like Google Docs to handle millions of concurrent users. It was this architectural revolution that truly separated the fleeting ASPs from the enduring SaaS empires.

CHAPTER FOUR: The Subscription Economy: A New Business Paradigm

The architectural revolution of multi-tenancy provided the engine for the cloud, but it was a radical shift in the commercial relationship between vendor and customer that provided the fuel. Technology alone, no matter how elegant, could not have powered the rise of the cloud empires. The true disruption came from pairing this new architecture with an equally new business philosophy, one that threw out the decades-old rulebook of software sales. The old world was built on a single, momentous transaction: the perpetual license. The new world would be built on a continuous, evolving relationship: the subscription. This was not merely a new pricing scheme; it was a fundamental re-imagining of value, turning software from a product you bought into a service you used.

For generations, the enterprise software industry had operated on a model that mirrored the sale of physical goods. A company would decide it needed a new accounting system or a CRM platform and would enter a long, arduous sales cycle. This process culminated in the payment of a massive, one-time fee to license the software in perpetuity. The customer "owned" the right to use that specific version of the software forever. This transaction was the climax of the relationship. Once the check was cashed and the software installed, the vendor's primary incentive structure shifted. Their focus moved on to the next big deal, leaving the customer with a complex piece of technology that was now their responsibility to manage, maintain, and extract value from.

This model created a feast-or-famine dynamic for software companies. Revenue was "lumpy," characterized by a frantic scramble at the end of every fiscal quarter to close as many large deals as possible to meet Wall Street's expectations. The health of the business was measured in massive, discrete chunks. This led to a culture of high-pressure sales tactics and a significant disconnect between the promises made during the sales cycle and the actual experience of using the software. Furthermore, the vendor's financial success was not directly tied to the customer's success. A customer could purchase a million-dollar software license, only to have the implementation project fail or the software gather dust on a server—a phenomenon derisively known as "shelfware." The software vendor, however, had already booked the revenue. Their only other significant revenue stream came from annual maintenance contracts, which entitled the customer to technical support and periodic, cumbersome upgrades to new versions of the software.

The subscription model turned this entire dynamic on its head. Instead of a large upfront payment, customers paid a smaller, recurring fee, typically on a monthly or annual basis. This simple change had profound consequences. The financial event was no longer a single explosion of cash but a steady, predictable stream. For the software company, this meant the end of the lumpy, quarter-end panic. They could now forecast their revenue with a remarkable degree of accuracy, a quality that investors and public markets would come to adore. This predictable income stream allowed for more stable, long-term planning in product development, hiring, and expansion.

This new model necessitated a new vocabulary. The boardrooms of Silicon Valley began to obsess over a new set of acronyms that would define the health and viability of a SaaS business. The most important of these was ARR, or Annual Recurring Revenue. This became the north star metric, representing the total value of all active subscriptions over a twelve-month period. It was a direct measure of the company's momentum and scale. Watching the ARR grow month over month was like watching a snowball roll downhill, gathering mass and velocity. It was the lifeblood of the subscription economy.

However, if ARR was the measure of success, its mortal enemy was churn. Churn is the rate at which customers cancel their subscriptions. In the old perpetual license world, a customer couldn't really "churn" in the same way; they owned the software. But in the subscription world, the customer was making a renewed purchasing decision every single month or year. If the service failed to deliver value, if the user experience was poor, or if a better alternative emerged, the customer could simply walk away. A high churn rate was a fatal leak in the bucket; no matter how fast a company poured new customers in the top, a leaky bucket would never fill. Minimizing churn became a paramount obsession, forcing companies to stay relentlessly focused on customer satisfaction.

This new reality gave rise to two other critical metrics that, when viewed together, could predict the future of any SaaS business: Customer Lifetime Value (LTV) and Customer Acquisition Cost (CAC). LTV represents the total amount of revenue a company can expect to generate from a single customer over the entire duration of their relationship. It's a function of the subscription price and the churn rate. CAC, on the other hand, is the total cost of sales and marketing required to land one new customer. The magic formula was simple: the LTV had to be significantly higher than the CAC. A healthy SaaS business might aim for an LTV that is at least three times its CAC. This ratio became the fundamental unit of economic viability, a clear signal that the business model was scalable and profitable.

For the customer, the subscription model was equally transformative, especially from a financial perspective. It represented a massive shift from Capital Expenditures (CapEx) to Operating Expenditures (OpEx). Under the old model, buying a major enterprise software package was a huge capital investment. The cost had to be formally approved, budgeted for far in advance, and then the asset—the software license—had to be depreciated on the company's balance sheet over several years. It was a slow, bureaucratic process that favored large, established companies with deep pockets. The subscription model changed the game entirely. The cost of the software was no longer a massive capital outlay but a predictable, monthly operating expense, much like the company's utility bill or office rent. This made it vastly easier for department heads to get approval and for finance teams to manage their budgets.

This financial agility fundamentally democratized access to powerful technology. A small, ten-person startup could now afford the same sophisticated CRM, marketing automation, or accounting software as a Fortune 500 giant. They didn't need to raise a round of venture funding just to buy a software license. They could simply sign up with a credit card and pay for the ten "seats" they needed. As the company grew, they could seamlessly add more seats. If they had to downsize, they could reduce their subscription accordingly. This elasticity removed the immense financial risk and friction associated with acquiring new technology, leveling the playing field and fueling a new era of innovation and competition.

Beyond the financials, the subscription model forged an entirely new kind of relationship between the vendor and the customer. The sale was no longer the finish line; it was the starting line. Because the customer could churn at any time, the vendor was now in the position of having to continuously re-earn their business, month after month. The focus had to shift from closing the deal to ensuring the customer was actively using the product and achieving their desired outcomes. This was a seismic cultural shift. The vendor's success was now inextricably linked to the customer's success. An unused license was no longer "shelfware"; it was a cancellation risk.

This dynamic forced the invention of an entirely new corporate function: Customer Success. This went far beyond traditional customer support, which was typically a reactive function designed to fix things that were broken. Customer Success was proactive. Its mission was to onboard new customers effectively, ensure they were trained, monitor their usage of the product to identify those who might be struggling, and proactively reach out to share best practices and help them unlock more value. This continuous engagement became critical for retention and also opened up new avenues for growth through upselling (convincing a customer to upgrade to a more expensive tier) and cross-selling (convincing them to buy additional products).

Of course, the transition wasn't without its psychological hurdles. In the early days, many businesses were wary of the idea of "renting" software. The concept of ownership was deeply ingrained. What if the SaaS company went out of business? Where would their data go? The notion of entrusting a company's most critical data to a third-party server in the nebulous "cloud" felt risky. The spectacular failures of the ASPs had left deep scars on the market's psyche. It took the steady, reliable performance of pioneers like Salesforce to gradually build trust and demonstrate that the benefits of the service model—the lower costs, the constant innovation, the freedom from maintenance—far outweighed the perceived risks of non-ownership.

Ultimately, the subscription model proved to be a more honest and aligned way of doing business. It forced software companies to build better products and provide better service because their revenue depended on it. It gave customers more power and flexibility than they had ever had before. The slow, infrequent upgrade cycle of the on-premise world was replaced by a continuous stream of small, incremental improvements delivered automatically over the cloud. The software was no longer a static asset that began aging the moment it was installed; it was a living, breathing service that was constantly evolving and getting better. This fundamental change in the economic and relational DNA of the software industry was the crucial paradigm shift that allowed the cloud empires to truly take root and flourish.

CHAPTER FIVE: The Rise of the Tech Giants: AWS, Azure, and Google Cloud

The multi-tenant architecture and the subscription business model created the two powerful currents that would carry the SaaS revolution forward. But for these currents to flow, they needed a riverbed. For a SaaS company to serve thousands of customers from a single application, it needed a place to run that application—a place with near-infinite computing power, cavernous storage, and lightning-fast networking, all available on demand. The early pioneers like Salesforce had to build this foundational layer themselves, a Herculean and expensive task of buying servers, leasing data center space, and managing complex infrastructure. This reality was a significant barrier, preventing a thousand other SaaS ideas from ever getting off the ground. For the cloud to truly become an empire for the many, it first needed an empire of infrastructure, built by giants.

This next, crucial layer of the cloud stack would come to be known as Infrastructure as a Service, or IaaS. If SaaS was about renting a finished application, IaaS was about renting the raw building blocks of computing itself. It was the digital equivalent of leasing a plot of land and having instant access to electricity, water, and gas hookups. You still had to build the house—the application, the database, the operating system—but you no longer had to generate the power or lay the pipes. This abstraction of the deepest layers of technology would unleash a torrent of innovation, and its origins, fittingly, came from a company that had mastered the art of infrastructure at a global scale: Amazon.

In the early 2000s, Amazon was not a technology company in the way we think of it today; it was the world's biggest online bookstore, a retailer grappling with the immense technical challenges of hyper-growth. To manage its sprawling e-commerce operation, Amazon's engineers had become exceptionally good at building scalable, reliable, and cost-effective internal systems. They had developed a set of common infrastructure services that any internal team could use, which radically sped up the process of launching new features and products. A small team, including Benjamin Black and Chris Pinkham, wrote a paper envisioning a future where Amazon's infrastructure was completely standardized and automated. Around 2003, the company's leadership, including a rising executive named Andy Jassy, realized that the powerful internal tools they had built to solve their own problems could be a product in their own right.

The idea was revolutionary: what if Amazon could offer its infrastructure as a service to the public, allowing any developer or company to access the same powerful and elastic computing resources that Amazon itself used? After a few years of internal development, this idea became a reality. In March 2006, Amazon Web Services (AWS) officially launched its first major service, the Simple Storage Service (S3). S3 did one thing, but it did it exceptionally well: it offered nearly infinite, highly durable, and inexpensive object storage, accessible via a simple web API. For the first time, a developer didn't need to buy and manage a storage server; they could just make an API call and store their data in Amazon's cloud, paying only for the gigabytes they used.

A few months later, in August 2006, AWS launched the service that would truly define the IaaS revolution: the Elastic Compute Cloud, or EC2. EC2 allowed users to rent virtual computers, known as "instances," by the hour. With a few clicks in a web console or a simple API call, a developer could spin up a virtual server running Linux or Windows, deploy their application, and have it running in minutes. When they were done, they could simply shut it down and stop paying. This was a mind-bending departure from the old world, where procuring a new server could take weeks or months of purchase orders, shipping, and physical installation. AWS had effectively turned hardware into software, a commodity to be consumed on demand.

The impact was immediate and profound. Startups, in particular, flocked to the new platform. It completely altered the economics of starting a technology company. Instead of needing to raise a large seed round to buy expensive Dell or HP servers, a founder could now launch their business with just a credit card, paying a few dollars an hour for the AWS resources they needed. This dramatically lowered the barrier to entry, fueling the "Lean Startup" movement and leading to an explosion of new web companies. Early adopters like SmugMug and Justin.tv (which would later become Twitch) were vocal evangelists, showcasing how they were building highly scalable businesses on the back of AWS, saving hundreds of thousands of dollars in upfront hardware costs.

For over half a decade, AWS operated with virtually no serious competition. It was a classic "first mover" advantage, and they used the time to relentlessly expand their service catalog, adding databases (RDS), networking tools (VPC), and countless other services. They also pioneered a culture of radical price reduction, consistently lowering the cost of their services as they achieved greater economies of scale. This created a virtuous cycle: lower prices attracted more customers, which led to more usage, which in turn allowed AWS to build more infrastructure and further lower its prices. By the time the rest of the tech world woke up to the scale of the opportunity, AWS was the undisputed king of the cloud, with a commanding market share.

The first giant to mount a serious challenge was Microsoft. The company had initially been slow to recognize the threat of the cloud, focused as it was on protecting its enormously profitable on-premise empire of Windows Server and Office. But by the late 2000s, it was clear that a paradigm shift was underway. Under the direction of Ray Ozzie, Microsoft began work on its own cloud platform, codenamed "Project Red Dog." It was officially announced in 2008 and became commercially available in February 2010 as Windows Azure.

Initially, Azure was more of a Platform as a Service (PaaS), designed to be the best place to run .NET web applications, rather than a direct IaaS competitor to AWS. It was a more prescriptive environment, an extension of the familiar Windows development world into the cloud. Early reviews were often harsh, comparing it unfavorably to the breadth and flexibility of AWS. However,

Microsoft possessed a colossal strategic advantage: its deep, decades-long relationships with nearly every enterprise IT department on the planet. Millions of businesses already ran on Microsoft software, and the company knew how to sell to them.

The real turning point for Microsoft's cloud ambitions came in 2014 with the appointment of Satya Nadella as CEO. Nadella had previously run the company's cloud and enterprise division and understood better than anyone that the future of Microsoft depended on a dramatic pivot. One of his first major acts was to rename "Windows Azure" to "Microsoft Azure," a symbolic but powerful signal that the platform was no longer just for Windows. It was to be a truly open, hybrid platform that embraced open-source technologies like Linux, which it had once famously derided.

Under Nadella's "cloud-first, mobile-first" mantra, Microsoft went all-in on Azure. They aggressively leveraged their existing enterprise agreements, making it easy and financially attractive for their massive customer base to start using Azure services. They developed a compelling "hybrid cloud" strategy with offerings like Azure Stack and later Azure Arc, which allowed companies to manage their on-premise servers and their cloud resources from a single control plane—a crucial feature for large corporations not yet ready to abandon their own data centers completely. This enterprise-friendly approach worked. Azure began to grow at a blistering pace, steadily closing the market share gap with AWS. The cloud was no longer a one-horse race.

The third giant to enter the fray was Google. On paper, Google should have been the first and most dominant player in cloud computing. Since its inception, the company had been building and running one of the most sophisticated, planet-scale computing infrastructures the world had ever seen to power its search engine, Gmail, and YouTube. They had pioneered many of the core concepts of distributed computing, with legendary internal systems like the Google File System, MapReduce, and Borg (the precursor to Kubernetes). The problem was that this infrastructure was a jealously guarded internal secret, a competitive advantage not to be shared with the outside world.

Google's first foray into the public cloud was in April 2008 with the launch of Google App Engine, a PaaS offering similar to the initial version of Azure. It allowed developers to build and host web applications on Google's infrastructure, but it was a relatively constrained environment. While technically impressive, it failed to gain the broad traction of AWS's more flexible IaaS model. For years, Google's cloud efforts seemed to be a side project, lacking the focused, all-in commitment of Amazon and, later, Microsoft.

The shift began in earnest around 2015, when Google hired Diane Greene, a co-founder of VMware and a legend in the enterprise software world, to lead its cloud business. This signaled a new seriousness about competing for large enterprise customers. Google Cloud Platform, or GCP, began to build out its IaaS offerings to be more directly comparable with AWS and Azure, while also playing to its unique strengths.

GCP's primary differentiators grew out of its parent company's DNA: data and networking. They offered world-class services in data analytics and machine learning, with groundbreaking products like BigQuery, a serverless data warehouse that could query petabytes of data in seconds. For companies looking to harness the power of AI and big data, GCP presented a compelling value proposition. Google also leveraged its massive global fiber network to offer premium networking performance. While it started from a distant third place in terms of market share, its technical excellence in key areas and a renewed focus on enterprise sales helped it carve out a significant niche and begin to grow rapidly.

By the late 2010s, the foundational layer of the cloud had been firmly established by these three titans. The resulting competition was fierce and hugely beneficial for the entire SaaS ecosystem. The "cloud wars" led to a continuous downward pressure on prices for core resources like compute and storage, making it ever cheaper to build and run a SaaS application. It also sparked a frantic race to innovate, with each provider constantly releasing new features and higher-level services, from managed Kubernetes clusters to serverless computing functions and sophisticated AI APIs. The giants had laid the railroad tracks, and now, any developer with an idea could build a train and reach a global audience, standing on the shoulders of the empires of infrastructure.

CHAPTER SIX: The API Economy: Building Interconnected Ecosystems

If the first era of cloud software was defined by standalone SaaS applications that liberated businesses from the tyranny of on-premise installations, the second era was defined by a single, transformative question: what if these applications could talk to each other? A company might use Salesforce for its customer data, Mailchimp for its newsletters, Zendesk for its support tickets, and Slack for its internal communication. Each was a powerful tool in its own right, a cloud-based island of efficiency. But the true power, the next great leap in productivity, would come from building bridges between these islands. This was the dawn of the API economy, a new phase of the cloud revolution where the value of a service was measured not just by what it did, but by how well it connected to everything else.

The digital bridge that makes this possible is the Application Programming Interface, or API. At its core, an API is simply a set of rules and definitions that allows one piece of software to request services or information from another. It is the invisible contract that governs these machine-to-machine conversations. A useful analogy is a waiter in a restaurant. You, the customer, don't need to know how the kitchen is organized, what brand of oven is being used, or the specific recipe for the dish you want. You simply consult the menu (the API documentation), give a clearly defined order to the waiter (the API call), and the waiter returns with your food (the data or service you requested). The API is this intermediary, abstracting away all the underlying complexity so that two systems can interact in a predictable and standardized way.

This concept stood in stark contrast to the old on-premise world, which was dominated by monolithic software suites. Giants like Oracle and SAP built their empires by offering a single, all-encompassing system that promised to do everything: finance, human resources, manufacturing, and customer management. The value proposition was integration, but it was an integration born of captivity. All the modules worked together because they were built by the same company and lived in the same digital fortress. This approach created deep vendor lock-in and often meant settling for a mediocre module in one area to get the benefit of a seamless connection to another.

The rise of specialized, "best-of-breed" SaaS applications shattered this model. A business could now pick the absolute best tool for each specific job. The challenge, however, was that this created a new kind of fragmentation. Customer data in the CRM needed to be synchronized with the email marketing list. A new sale logged in the accounting software needed to trigger a project in the team collaboration tool. Without a way to connect these services, employees were forced into the soul-crushing work of manual data entry, constantly copying and pasting information from one browser tab to another. The API was the cure for this digital disease, the universal translator that allowed a diverse ecosystem of applications to function as a cohesive whole.

While many SaaS companies gradually added APIs as a feature, a new breed of cloud empire emerged that was "API-first." These companies built their entire business not around a graphical user interface for humans, but around a programmatic interface for developers. Their product *was* the API. Perhaps the most iconic of these pioneers is Twilio. Founded in 2008, Twilio recognized that while telecommunications infrastructure was messy and complex, the basic functions—making a phone call or sending a text message—could be reduced to a few simple lines of code. Instead of building a user-facing app, they built a powerful set of APIs that allowed any developer to embed communications directly into their own software. Suddenly, a company like Uber didn't need to become a telecom expert to let drivers and riders call each other; they could just use the Twilio API. Twilio's business model was pure utility: you paid for what you used, per text message or per minute of voice call.

Another titan of the API-first world is Stripe, founded in 2010. At the time, accepting payments online was a notoriously difficult process, requiring businesses to navigate a labyrinth of merchant accounts, payment gateways, and arcane security compliance. Stripe's founders, the Collison brothers, boiled this entire complex process down to a clean, well-documented API. With just a few lines of code, a developer could integrate a secure and reliable payment system into any website or application. Like Twilio, Stripe's interface was for machines, not humans, and its revenue model was based on taking a small percentage of each transaction it processed. These companies proved that you could build a multi-billion dollar empire by selling not a finished product, but the powerful building blocks that other companies could use to innovate.

For more traditional SaaS companies, opening up an API transformed their product into a platform. No company understood this better than Salesforce. With the launch of the AppExchange in 2005, Salesforce used its APIs to invite third-party developers to build and sell their own applications that integrated with and extended the core Salesforce CRM. This was a masterstroke of strategy. It unleashed a wave of innovation that Salesforce could never have produced on its own. Need a specialized tool for the construction industry or a sophisticated document signing integration? There was an app for that on the AppExchange. This created a powerful network effect: more customers attracted more developers, who built more apps, which made the platform more valuable and attracted more customers. The API became a strategic moat, making the Salesforce platform stickier and far more difficult for competitors to displace.

The explosion of the API economy was accelerated by a crucial technological shift. Early attempts at system integration often relied on complex and rigid protocols like SOAP (Simple Object Access Protocol), which were cumbersome to work with. The breakthrough came with the widespread adoption of REST (Representational State Transfer), an architectural style proposed in 2000 by Roy Fielding, one of the authors of the HTTP protocol that powers the web. REST wasn't a strict protocol but a set of principles that used the existing, familiar verbs of the web—like GET, POST, PUT, and DELETE—to interact with resources. This, combined with lightweight data formats like JSON (JavaScript Object Notation), made creating and consuming APIs dramatically simpler and more accessible to millions of developers. It was a democratization of integration.

However, as the average company began to subscribe to dozens of different SaaS applications, a new problem emerged: integration chaos. Even with simple REST APIs, building and maintaining custom, point-to-point connections between every single app became a brittle and unmanageable mess, a digital ball of spaghetti. A change to one application's API could break a dozen different connections. This complexity created the opportunity for yet another layer in the cloud stack: the Integration Platform as a Service, or iPaaS.

iPaaS solutions act as a central switchboard for the cloud, providing pre-built connectors and visual tools that allow companies to build, manage, and monitor the flow of data between their various applications. This market itself split into two main camps. On one end were user-friendly workflow automation tools like Zapier. Zapier empowered non-technical users to create simple "if this, then that" automations, connecting thousands of popular web apps with a few clicks. For example, "when a new row is added to a Google Sheet, create a new contact in HubSpot." It was a powerful tool for automating the routine tasks of digital work.

On the other end of the spectrum were enterprise-grade iPaaS platforms like MuleSoft (which Salesforce would acquire for a staggering $6.5 billion in 2018) and Dell Boomi. These platforms were designed for complex, mission-critical integrations, handling high-volume data transformations and connecting not just cloud apps, but also deeply entrenched on-premise and legacy systems. They were the heavy-duty plumbing for the modern enterprise, managed by IT departments to ensure security and reliability across a hybrid cloud environment. The rise of iPaaS demonstrated that the API economy had matured to the point where the connections themselves had become a product.

This new landscape fundamentally changed business strategy. The ability to connect to an ecosystem became as important as the features of the core product. Companies began to monetize their APIs directly through various models: pay-as-you-go based on the number of API calls, subscription tiers for different levels of access, or even revenue-sharing agreements. More broadly, the API economy enabled entire businesses to be built by cleverly combining existing services. An entrepreneur could launch a new e-commerce service by stitching together Stripe for payments, Shopify for the storefront, Algolia for search, and a logistics provider's API for shipping. This modular approach dramatically lowered the cost and time required to bring new digital products to market.

The API economy represents the maturation of the cloud. It is the realization that software, like the internet itself, derives its power from connection, not isolation. It transformed standalone applications into a vast, interconnected network, a digital ecosystem where data could flow freely to automate processes, generate insights, and create entirely new forms of value. The empires of the cloud were no longer just destinations; they had become platforms, foundational layers upon which a new generation of innovation could be built.

CHAPTER SEVEN: Data as the New Gold: Analytics, AI, and Machine Learning in SaaS

The great migration to the cloud had an unforeseen and profoundly valuable side effect. In the on-premise world, every company's data was an isolated island, locked away in a private server room. But the multi-tenant architecture of SaaS, by its very nature, funneled the operational data of thousands, and eventually millions, of businesses into centralized systems. Every click, every entry, every saved record, and every closed deal from every customer created a constant stream of information. This torrent of digital detritus, initially seen as a simple byproduct of running the service, came to be known as "data exhaust." It didn't take long for SaaS providers to realize they weren't just running software; they were sitting on a digital gold mine. The data itself, once aggregated, anonymized, and analyzed, could be refined into a new and potent form of value: intelligence.

The first and most obvious use for this newfound treasure was internal. For the first time, software vendors had a perfect, real-time window into how their products were actually being used. In the old world of shrink-wrapped software, a company like Microsoft might spend millions on focus groups and user surveys to guess which features people liked in Microsoft Word. A SaaS company, by contrast, could simply look at the data. They could see with absolute clarity which features were used every day, which were ignored, where users were getting stuck in the workflow, and how long it took to complete certain tasks. This created a powerful feedback loop, allowing for a data-driven approach to product development that was impossible in the on-premise era. Product roadmaps were no longer based on the loudest customer's demands or a senior executive's intuition; they were shaped by the collective behavior of the entire user base.

Soon, this capability was turned outward, offered back to the customers themselves as a core feature. The first wave of this was the rise of built-in business intelligence (BI) and analytics. SaaS applications evolved from simple systems of record—places to store information—into systems of insight. A CRM was no longer just a digital rolodex; it was a command center with dashboards that visualized a sales team's pipeline, win rates, and quarterly performance. A marketing automation platform didn't just send emails; it provided detailed reports on open rates, click-throughs, and campaign return on investment. This was a significant value-add. Customers were no longer just renting the software; they were renting access to a tool that helped them understand their own business better.

The true magic, however, came from a unique benefit that only a multi-tenant SaaS provider could offer: benchmarking. Because the vendor held the data for thousands of companies, they could anonymize and aggregate it to provide powerful comparative insights. A user of a SaaS accounting tool could now see not just their own company's profit margin, but how that margin compared to the average for other companies of a similar size in their specific industry. A marketing manager could learn that their email campaign's open rate of 15% was actually below the industry benchmark of 22%, signaling a need for improvement. This was something on-premise software could never do. It was a compelling new reason to choose a SaaS solution, transforming the vendor from a simple tool provider into a source of strategic business intelligence.

As the volume and velocity of this data exploded, the traditional relational databases that powered most applications began to strain under the analytical load. Running a massive, complex query to generate a report could slow down the application for everyone else. This created the need for a new kind of cloud infrastructure, one designed specifically for large-scale data analysis: the cloud data warehouse. This was a specialized type of database optimized for reading and analyzing colossal datasets, a place where a company could consolidate information from dozens of different sources for a holistic view of their operations.

The undisputed pioneer in this new category was Snowflake. Founded in 2012 by former Oracle database architects, Snowflake's platform was revolutionary because it was the first data warehouse built from the ground up for the cloud. Its killer feature was the separation of storage and compute. This meant that a company could store a petabyte of data very cheaply, and then spin up massive clusters of computing power to analyze it for a few hours, shutting them down (and stopping the billing) when the work was done. This elastic, pay-for-what-you-use model was perfectly suited to the variable demands of data analytics. Alongside offerings from the big three infrastructure providers— Amazon Redshift, Google BigQuery, and Microsoft's Azure Synapse Analytics—the cloud data warehouse became the central repository for the modern enterprise's data.

The rise of these powerful data warehouses, in turn, fueled another wave of specialized SaaS companies. Firms like Looker (acquired by Google for $2.6 billion) and Tableau (acquired by Salesforce for a staggering $15.7 billion) built their entire businesses not on generating new data, but on providing beautiful, intuitive, and powerful tools to explore and visualize the data residing in these new warehouses. They were the sophisticated lens through which businesses could finally make sense of the mountains of information they were collecting from their various SaaS tools and internal systems. A company could now pipe data from its Salesforce CRM, its Marketo marketing platform, and its NetSuite ERP system into a single Snowflake instance, and then use Tableau to build a unified dashboard for its CEO, providing a single, real-time view of the entire business.

With the ability to collect, store, and visualize vast amounts of historical data, the next logical step in the evolution was to stop looking in the rearview mirror and start looking through the windshield. The industry began to shift its focus from descriptive analytics (what happened?) to the far more valuable realm of predictive analytics (what will happen?). This leap was made possible by the infusion of Artificial Intelligence (AI) and, more specifically, a subfield called Machine Learning (ML).

The concept was straightforward. The massive, clean, and well-structured datasets aggregated by SaaS providers were the perfect fuel for training machine learning models. A model could be fed historical data and learn to recognize the subtle patterns that preceded a particular outcome. For example, by analyzing tens of thousands of past sales deals—some won, some lost—an ML model could learn the characteristics of a lead that was most likely to convert into a paying customer. It could identify factors invisible to a human, such as the ideal number of email exchanges, the optimal time between a demo and a follow-up call, or the job title of the decision-maker that correlated most highly with success.

SaaS vendors began embedding this predictive intelligence directly into their products, transforming them from passive tools into proactive advisors. Salesforce was a leader in this charge with the launch of its "Einstein" AI layer. Suddenly, Salesforce wasn't just showing a salesperson their list of leads; it was scoring those leads, automatically highlighting the ones that deserved immediate attention. It could recommend the "next best action" to move a deal forward or analyze a team's pipeline to produce a sales forecast that was often more accurate than the sales manager's own gut feeling.

This pattern was replicated across the SaaS landscape. In the world of customer support, a system like Zendesk could use ML to analyze the text of an incoming support ticket and automatically route it to the agent with the most relevant expertise. A human resources platform from Workday could analyze employee data to predict which high-performing individuals might be a flight risk, allowing managers to intervene proactively. Even in the consumer space, this was the engine behind Netflix's uncanny ability to recommend your next binge-watch or Spotify's perfectly curated "Discover Weekly" playlist. The software was no longer just executing commands; it was anticipating needs.

Just as this predictive wave was cresting, a new, even more powerful form of AI exploded into the public consciousness: generative AI. Pioneered by research labs like OpenAI with its groundbreaking GPT series of models, this new technology represented a quantum leap. Unlike earlier AI, which was primarily focused on prediction and classification, these Large Language Models (LLMs) could understand and *generate* human-like text, images, code, and other content. This wasn't just about finding a needle in a haystack; it was about creating a new needle from scratch.

The impact on the SaaS world was immediate and seismic. The dominant metaphor for this new capability became the "copilot," an AI assistant embedded directly within an application, ready to help the user accomplish their goals. Microsoft, a major investor in OpenAI, aggressively integrated this technology across its entire product suite with Microsoft 365 Copilot. Now, a user in Microsoft Word could simply ask the AI to "write a draft of a proposal based on my notes from yesterday's meeting." In Outlook, it could summarize a long email thread and draft a polite reply. In PowerPoint, it could generate an entire presentation from a simple text prompt.

This generative capability is being woven into the fabric of virtually every major SaaS application. Marketing platforms can now automatically generate dozens of variations of ad copy and social media posts. CRMs can draft personalized follow-up emails for salespeople. Software development tools can write entire blocks of code based on a developer's plain-English description of the desired function. This fundamentally changes the user interface. Instead of navigating complex menus and clicking buttons, users can increasingly interact with software through natural language, simply telling the application what they want to achieve. It is a shift from a graphical user interface (GUI) to a language user interface (LUI).

This evolution from basic analytics to generative AI has cemented the role of data as the most important strategic asset in the cloud. It has given rise to a new and incredibly powerful competitive advantage known as a "data network effect." The mechanism is a self-reinforcing flywheel. A SaaS product with more users collects more data. This larger, more diverse dataset can be used to train a more accurate and capable AI model. The smarter, AI-powered features that result from this model make the product more valuable and attractive, which in turn brings in even more users. This cycle—more users, more data, better AI, more users—creates a formidable moat that is exceptionally difficult for new competitors to cross. A startup can copy a product's features, but they cannot copy the decade of proprietary data that makes the incumbent's AI smart. In the empire of the cloud, code may be king, but data, refined by the alchemy of artificial intelligence, has become the gold that funds the throne.

CHAPTER EIGHT: Security and Trust in the Cloud: Building Digital Fortresses

The entire premise of Software as a Service rested on a request that, in the early 2000s, sounded like corporate insanity: take your most valuable asset—your customer lists, your financial records, your strategic plans—and hand it over to a stranger on the internet. For a generation of business leaders and IT managers raised on the on-premise model, security was a physical concept. It was a locked server room, a blinking firewall appliance in a rack, the comforting hum of hardware that you owned and controlled within your own four walls. This provided a powerful, if sometimes illusory, sense of safety. The cloud asked them to trade this tangible security for a promise.

This psychological barrier was the single greatest obstacle to the adoption of SaaS. The spectacular failures of the first-wave ASPs, some of which vanished overnight taking their customers' data with them, had left a deep scar. Executives peppered early SaaS salespeople with a barrage of skeptical questions. What if your company goes out of business? Who else can see my data? What happens if you get hacked? How can I be sure my information is truly private when it's sitting on the same server as my competitor's? These were not trivial concerns; they were existential threats to the entire cloud model.

For the SaaS revolution to succeed, its pioneers had to do more than just build a better product; they had to engineer trust itself. They needed to construct a new kind of fortress, one whose walls were made not of concrete and steel, but of encryption, audits, and transparent policies. They had to convince the world that placing data in their professionally managed cloud was not a reckless act of faith, but a rational and, ultimately, far more secure decision than leaving it on an aging, forgotten server in an office closet. This meant shifting the conversation from a vague notion of "the cloud" to a concrete framework of controls and responsibilities.

At the heart of this new security paradigm is the "shared responsibility model," a concept that became the foundational agreement between cloud providers and their customers. The model delineates a clear boundary, defining who is responsible for what. In the world of Infrastructure as a Service (IaaS), the cloud provider—like AWS, Microsoft, or Google—is responsible for the security *of* the cloud. This includes the immense physical security of their data centers, the protection of the core network, and the integrity of the underlying hardware and virtualization software. The customer, in turn, is responsible for security *in* the cloud. This means they are responsible for configuring their virtual servers correctly, managing user access, patching their own operating systems, and encrypting their data.

For a SaaS provider, this model shifts slightly. The SaaS vendor essentially becomes the "customer" of the IaaS provider, inheriting the responsibility for everything from the operating system upwards. They are responsible for securing the application itself, protecting the data within it, and managing the infrastructure it runs on. The end customer's responsibility is then narrowed to two primary areas: managing their own users and their data. They decide who gets access to the service and with what level of permissions, and they are responsible for the content they upload. This clarity was crucial; it replaced fear and uncertainty with a well-defined set of roles, allowing businesses to understand and manage their specific areas of risk.

The first layer of this new digital fortress was the sheer physical security of the data centers operated by the IaaS giants, a level of protection that almost no individual company could hope to replicate. These are not your average office buildings. They are often anonymous, windowless structures surrounded by high fences, concrete barriers, and sophisticated intrusion detection systems. Access is controlled by a series of checkpoints, requiring biometric verification like fingerprint or iris scans. The facilities are monitored 24/7 by armed guards and countless security cameras. Inside, server cages are locked, and access is strictly logged and audited. These centers are also built to withstand natural disasters, with redundant power from multiple utility grids, massive diesel generators for backup, and sophisticated fire suppression systems. The SaaS provider, by building on top of this infrastructure, could credibly argue that a customer's data was physically safer in their cloud than in their own office.

On top of this physical foundation, SaaS vendors built layers of digital security. A primary focus was protecting data as it moved across the internet and as it sat idle on their servers. The first part, known as "encryption in transit," became standard practice. This is achieved through Transport Layer Security (TLS), the same technology that powers the padlock icon in a web browser. It creates a secure, encrypted tunnel between the user's computer and the SaaS application, ensuring that any data passing between them—passwords, financial information, customer details—is unreadable to anyone who might try to intercept it.

The second part, "encryption at rest," was just as critical. This involves encrypting the data when it is stored on disk drives within the data center. This ensures that even if an attacker were to somehow gain physical access to a hard drive—an incredibly unlikely scenario—the data on it would be a meaningless jumble of scrambled characters without the corresponding encryption keys. For multi-tenant applications, this was often coupled with the strict data segregation enforced by the Tenant ID. Each customer's data was not only logically separated by the application's code but also potentially encrypted with a unique key, adding another formidable barrier to prevent one customer from ever accessing another's information.

Of course, the most common way for an attacker to breach a system is not by physically breaking into a data center but by stealing a legitimate user's credentials. Consequently, securing the "front door" of the application became a paramount concern. This led to the widespread adoption of robust Identity and Access Management (IAM) controls. The most visible of these was Multi-Factor Authentication (MFA), which requires a user to provide a second form of verification—like a code from a mobile app or a physical security key—in addition to their password. While sometimes seen as a minor inconvenience, MFA is one of the single most effective security measures a company can implement, drastically reducing the risk of an account takeover.

For larger enterprise customers, managing hundreds of user accounts across dozens of different SaaS applications presented a new kind of security nightmare. To solve this, the industry embraced Single Sign-On (SSO) solutions, often provided by specialized SaaS security companies like Okta. SSO allows a company's IT department to manage user access centrally. An employee can log in once with their corporate credentials and gain access to all their approved SaaS applications without having to remember dozens of different passwords. When that employee leaves the company, the IT department can revoke their access to everything with a single click. This was a win-win: it improved the user experience while giving corporations the centralized control and security they desperately needed.

However, promises of advanced technology were not enough to build trust. The market demanded proof. This need gave rise to a cottage industry of auditors and a whole new language of compliance certifications. These certifications became the currency of trust, a way for a SaaS provider to demonstrate through an independent third party that they had the necessary controls in place to protect customer data. Without them, selling to any reasonably-sized business became nearly impossible.

The most important of these in the North American market became the SOC 2 (Service Organization Control 2) report. A SOC 2 audit, performed by a certified public accounting firm, involves a deep and lengthy examination of a provider's systems and processes against a set of criteria known as the Trust Services Criteria: Security, Availability, Processing Integrity, Confidentiality, and Privacy. Receiving a "clean" SOC 2 report became a rite of passage for any serious SaaS company, a tangible piece of evidence they could provide to prospective customers to allay their security fears.

The global equivalent that gained prominence was ISO/IEC 27001, an international standard that specifies the requirements for establishing, implementing, maintaining, and continually improving an information security management system (ISMS). Achieving ISO 27001 certification signaled to the world that a company had a formal, risk-based, and comprehensive approach to security that met a globally recognized benchmark.

On top of these general security frameworks, SaaS providers targeting specific industries had to meet even more stringent, domain-specific regulations. For any company handling healthcare information in the United States, compliance with the Health Insurance Portability and Accountability Act (HIPAA) was non-negotiable. This required implementing specific administrative, physical, and technical safeguards to protect patient data. Similarly, the introduction of the General Data Protection Regulation (GDPR) in Europe in 2018 set a new global standard for data privacy, imposing strict rules on how the personal data of EU citizens could be collected, processed, and stored, with massive fines for non-compliance. SaaS vendors who wanted to operate in these lucrative markets had no choice but to build their platforms and processes to meet these exacting standards, a process that ultimately raised the security and privacy bar for the entire industry.

Despite all these technological and procedural safeguards, the cloud security landscape is a constant cat-and-mouse game. The weakest link in the chain is often not the technology but the human element. Attackers quickly realized that it was far easier to trick an employee into giving up their password than it was to breach a well-defended cloud data center. This led to the rise of sophisticated phishing attacks—deceptive emails designed to look legitimate in order to steal credentials—and other forms of social engineering. The shared responsibility model became critical here; a SaaS provider could implement MFA, but it was up to the customer to enforce its use and to train their employees to recognize and report these kinds of threats.

The complexity of securing these new cloud environments also created a market opportunity that the SaaS world was only too happy to fill. An entire new ecosystem of "security SaaS" companies emerged, offering specialized tools to help businesses manage the cloud's new security challenges. Companies like CrowdStrike offered cloud-based endpoint protection to replace traditional antivirus software. Firms like Zscaler provided a secure web gateway in the cloud, inspecting a company's internet traffic for threats without needing a physical appliance. The cloud, in a sense, began generating its own antibodies, creating new layers of protection that were themselves delivered as a service, further cementing the model's dominance. The fortress of trust was never truly finished; it was, and remains, a structure under constant renovation, with new defenses being added daily to counter the ever-evolving tactics of those who would seek to breach its walls.

CHAPTER NINE: The User Experience (UX) Imperative: Design-Centric SaaS

For decades, the users of enterprise software were a captive audience. The software they were forced to use at work was not chosen by them, but for them. The decision was made in a distant boardroom by a chief information officer or an IT committee whose primary concerns were security, scalability, and how well the purchase would integrate with the company's existing Oracle database. The actual experience of the human being who had to spend eight hours a day clicking through its menus was, at best, a secondary consideration. The result was a generation of tools that were powerful in function but punishing in form.

This was the era of the "gray box." Enterprise software was a landscape of drab, cluttered interfaces, nonsensical workflows, and an endless proliferation of buttons, tabs, and drop-down menus. Applications from giants like SAP, Siebel, or PeopleSoft were infamous for their steep learning curves, often requiring days or even weeks of mandatory training just to perform basic tasks. The software was built like a battleship: immensely capable, but slow, complex, and requiring a specialized crew to operate. It was a world of feature bloat, where the value of a product was often measured by the sheer length of its feature list, regardless of whether those features were discoverable or even useful. The user was expected to adapt to the software, not the other way around.

Then, starting in the mid-2000s, a quiet revolution in user expectation began, not in the office, but in the home and in the pocket. The launch of the iPhone in 2007 was a watershed moment. It placed a beautifully designed, incredibly intuitive computer in the hands of hundreds of millions of people. Alongside this, web applications from companies like Google and Facebook set a new standard for digital interaction. Searching the entire internet was as simple as typing in a single box. Connecting with friends involved a clean, endlessly scrolling feed. These consumer-grade experiences were fast, elegant, and required no instruction manual. They just worked.

This phenomenon became known as the "consumerization of IT." People would spend their evenings using delightful applications on their phones and then arrive at work on Monday morning to confront the gray, soul-crushing interfaces of their professional tools. The contrast was jarring and deeply frustrating. A powerful, bottom-up pressure began to build. Employees started asking their managers and IT departments, "Why is our work software so terrible? Why can't it be as easy to use as my phone?" This was a question the on-premise software giants were ill-equipped to answer. Their entire business model was built on selling to the executive, not delighting the end user.

This shift in expectation perfectly converged with the rise of the SaaS business model, and the result was explosive. The subscription model fundamentally changed who the software had to please. In the old world, a company would make a massive, multi-million dollar, multi-year commitment to an on-premise system. Once that check was cashed, the users were stuck with it, for better or worse. In the SaaS world, the purchasing decision was often decentralized and continuous. A single team could decide to try a new project management tool by putting it on a credit card for fifty dollars a month. The user was no longer a captive; they were a customer, one who could cancel their subscription at any time.

This new reality made the user experience a matter of life and death for a SaaS company. If the software was confusing, clunky, or frustrating, users would simply abandon it. A poor user experience didn't just lead to grumbling in the break room; it led directly to churn, the metric that could single-handedly kill a subscription business. Suddenly, the happiness and productivity of the individual user was not a "nice-to-have" feature; it was the single most important driver of customer retention and revenue. Design was no longer about applying a coat of paint at the end of the development cycle. It was a core, strategic imperative, baked into the product from the very beginning.

In a crowded market where the underlying cloud infrastructure was becoming a commodity, user experience emerged as the ultimate differentiator. Two companies could offer a product with the exact same list of features, but the one that was simpler, more intuitive, and more enjoyable to use would invariably win. This realization gave birth to a new generation of SaaS companies that were design-led from their inception. They understood that the product itself had to be the primary engine of its own growth.

This philosophy was crystallized in a new go-to-market strategy known as Product-Led Growth, or PLG. The PLG model, championed by companies like Slack, Dropbox, and Atlassian, flipped the traditional sales process on its head. Instead of a sales team trying to convince a CIO to buy the product from the top down, the PLG strategy focused on making the product so good that individual users would adopt it, love it, and then spread it organically throughout their organization from the bottom up. For this to work, the user experience had to be flawless.

The first five minutes of a user's interaction with the product became the most important battleground. This critical window was all the time a company had to demonstrate value and get the user to their "aha!" moment—the point where they truly grasped how the product could make their life better. This led to an obsessive focus on frictionless onboarding. Instead of dense manuals, SaaS products began using interactive tutorials, helpful tooltips, and cleverly designed "empty states" that guided the new user on what to do first. The goal was to eliminate every possible point of friction and make the path to value as short and as simple as possible.

The company that perhaps best exemplified this new design-centric approach was Slack. Before Slack, enterprise communication was dominated by the cluttered chaos of email and the arcane, clunky interfaces of early chat clients. Slack entered this space with a product that was not only functional but also fun. The interface was clean, colorful, and organized around intuitive channels. But it was the small details that revealed its design-led ethos. The satisfying "thwack" sound of a new message arriving, the ability to react to posts with a simple emoji, the playful and helpful personality of the Slackbot—all these elements were carefully crafted to create a positive emotional connection with the user. Slack didn't just help you communicate with your team; it made doing so feel less like work.

Another icon of the UX imperative was Dropbox. Its genius was in its invisibility. The user experience was so simple it was almost non-existent: a single, magical folder on your computer that automatically synchronized its contents across all your devices. There were no complex settings to configure or buttons to press. It just worked. This illusion of simplicity masked an immense amount of sophisticated engineering and design thinking, all focused on abstracting away the complexity of file synchronization and cloud storage. Dropbox won not by having the most features, but by providing the most seamless and effortless experience.

This relentless focus on the user also meant that design decisions could no longer be based on gut instinct alone. The new rule was: "You are not your user." SaaS companies became masters of data-driven design. They embedded analytics tools deep within their products to track user behavior in aggregate. They could see where users were clicking, how long they spent on certain tasks, and where they were dropping out of a workflow. This quantitative data was then combined with qualitative feedback from user interviews and usability testing. A/B testing, where two different versions of a design are shown to different segments of users to see which one performs better, became a standard practice for optimizing everything from the color of a button to the layout of an entire page.

This shift toward user-centricity forced a profound change in how SaaS companies were organized. Design was elevated from a service department to a strategic partner at the leadership table. Designers were no longer siloed artists brought in at the end; they were embedded within product teams from day one, working alongside product managers and engineers to define not just how the product looked, but how it behaved and what it should do. The rise of the Chief Design Officer as a key executive role signaled that the user's voice was now represented in the C-suite.

To manage the complexity of designing for multiple platforms and a rapidly evolving product, companies began creating comprehensive "design systems." These were not just simple style guides; they were extensive libraries of reusable components, patterns, and guidelines that governed the entire user interface. Systems like Google's Material Design, Salesforce's Lightning Design System, and Atlassian's Design System became the single source of truth for design within their organizations. They ensured a consistent and high-quality user experience across a sprawling suite of products, while also dramatically speeding up the development process. An engineer could now assemble a new interface from a palette of pre-built, pre-approved components, confident that the result would be both functional and on-brand.

This new imperative also cast a spotlight on the importance of accessibility, the practice of designing products that can be used by people with disabilities. What began as a moral and legal obligation turned out to be a catalyst for better design for everyone. The process of making an application navigable via a keyboard, compatible with screen readers, and designed with sufficient color contrast often resulted in a cleaner, more logical, and more flexible interface for all users.

In the end, the user experience imperative was the great humanization of enterprise software. It was the recognition that the people using these tools were not automatons but busy, often-stressed human beings who deserved tools that were respectful of their time and attention. The cloud empires that thrived were the ones that understood this fundamental truth. They realized that in a world of infinite choice, where the next competitor is just a click away, the surest path to building a loyal customer base and a durable business was to create a product that people genuinely loved to use. The gray box had been shattered, and in its place was a vibrant, user-centric landscape where design was no longer a luxury, but the very language of success.

CHAPTER TEN: Vertical SaaS: Conquering Niche Industries

For a decade, the great cloud empires were built horizontally. They forged broad, powerful tools designed to solve universal business problems that cut across every sector of the economy. A sales team is a sales team, whether they are selling software or cement. A marketing department needs to send emails, whether for a fashion brand or a financial firm. A finance team needs to close the books, regardless of the industry. This horizontal approach, championed by pioneers like Salesforce and NetSuite, was logical and immensely successful. It targeted the largest possible markets with tools that, by design, were meant to be a one-size-fits-all solution for a specific job function. The world needed a universal CRM, a universal accounting system, and a universal collaboration tool.

This first wave of SaaS created a new digital landscape, but it left vast territories of the economy relatively untouched. While a generic CRM was certainly better than a spreadsheet for a construction company, it didn't understand the unique language and labyrinthine processes of that industry. It had no concept of a subcontractor, a change order, or a request for information (RFI). The construction manager had to contort their real-world workflow to fit the rigid boxes of the horizontal software. This friction existed everywhere, in every industry that operated outside the clean, predictable confines of a typical tech company. Law firms, dental practices, wineries, trucking companies, and funeral homes all had highly specific, deeply entrenched ways of working that were poorly served by generic tools.

This gap between the horizontal giants and the complex reality of specialized industries created the single biggest opportunity in the second act of the SaaS revolution. A new breed of entrepreneur began to emerge, not from the ranks of pure technologists, but from the industries they sought to serve. They were former architects who were fed up with managing projects on a mountain of paper, or restaurant owners who knew there had to be a better way than juggling five different, disconnected systems to run their business. They understood a fundamental truth: while all businesses share some common functions, the most critical workflows are unique to their industry. They chose to build their empires not by spanning the entire map, but by drilling deep into a single, lucrative territory. This was the rise of vertical SaaS.

The distinction is simple but profound. Horizontal SaaS sells a tool for a job. Vertical SaaS sells a complete solution for an industry. It is the difference between a high-quality, general-purpose chef's knife and a complete, specialized toolkit designed for a sushi master. The chef's knife is useful in any kitchen, but the sushi toolkit contains not only the specialized knives but also the bamboo rolling mats and rice paddles—everything needed for that specific craft. A vertical SaaS platform aims to be the digital toolkit for its chosen industry, a single system of record that manages the entire core operation from start to finish.

This focused approach fundamentally rewrites the economics of building a software company. One of the most significant advantages is a dramatic reduction in the cost of acquiring a customer. A horizontal company like HubSpot must market its software to a vast and diverse audience of millions of businesses. Its marketing message must be broad enough to appeal to everyone, and it must compete for attention in the noisiest channels on the internet. A vertical SaaS company, by contrast, knows exactly who its customers are and where to find them. If you are building software for golf course management, your entire target market can be reached through a handful of industry trade magazines, a booth at the annual PGA Merchandise Show, and a targeted digital ad campaign aimed at people with the job title "Golf Course Superintendent." The marketing is precise, the language is specific, and the return on investment is often far higher.

Once a customer is won, they are significantly less likely to leave. This lower churn, or higher "stickiness," is another hallmark of the vertical model. Because the software is not just a peripheral tool but is deeply woven into the core operational fabric of the business, ripping it out and replacing it becomes a monumental task. For a dental practice, the vertical SaaS platform manages everything: patient scheduling, insurance billing, electronic health records, and X-ray imaging. To switch to a new system would mean retraining the entire staff and undertaking a complex data migration, all while trying to run a busy practice. The switching costs are immense. The software ceases to be a discretionary purchase and becomes the central nervous system of the company, as essential as the dental chairs themselves.

This deep integration and indispensability give vertical SaaS providers a third major advantage: greater pricing power. Businesses are willing to pay a premium for a solution that perfectly fits their needs, speaks their language, and solves their most complex, industry-specific problems. A generic tool might be cheaper, but the cost of the workarounds, the manual data entry, and the sheer inefficiency it creates often makes it a false economy. As a result, the average revenue per user (ARPU) is typically much higher for vertical solutions. When a company can prove that its software directly leads to greater efficiency, improved compliance, or higher revenue for its customers, it can command a price that reflects that immense value.

Perhaps the most celebrated example of this strategy in action is Veeva Systems. In the mid-2000s, the pharmaceutical industry was a massive, technology-starved market dominated by a few on-premise giants. Salesforce was the undisputed king of horizontal cloud CRM, but its generic platform struggled to meet the highly specific and heavily regulated needs of pharmaceutical sales and clinical trials. Peter Gassner, a former executive at Salesforce, saw this gap and founded Veeva in 2007. Instead of trying to reinvent the wheel, he made a brilliant strategic decision: he built his company *on top* of the Salesforce platform.

Veeva used the core Salesforce architecture but built a highly specialized application layer over it, designed exclusively for the life sciences industry. The Veeva CRM understood the unique relationships between pharmaceutical reps, doctors, and hospitals. It had built-in features for managing drug samples and reporting on physician interactions in a way that complied with complex government regulations. Gassner and his team didn't just sell software; they sold deep industry expertise. They understood the world of clinical data management, regulatory submissions to the Food and Drug Administration (FDA), and quality control in manufacturing. This allowed them to create a suite of interconnected products that became the de facto operating system for many of the world's largest pharmaceutical companies. A horizontal player like Salesforce could never have achieved this level of industry-specific depth on its own.

A similar story unfolded in the chaotic world of the restaurant industry. For years, restaurants were forced to patch together a clumsy assortment of technologies: a cash register from one vendor, a credit card terminal from another, a separate system for managing online orders, and a paper book for reservations. Toast, founded in 2011 by three former tech executives, set out to replace this mess with a single, elegant, all-in-one platform. They combined a modern, tablet-based point-of-sale (POS) system with integrated payment processing, online ordering, payroll management, and customer loyalty programs.

Toast's success was rooted in its obsessive focus on the restaurant workflow. They understood the difference between a quick-service cafe and a fine-dining establishment. Their hardware was designed to withstand the heat and spills of a busy kitchen. Their software included features specifically for splitting checks, managing tips, and sending orders directly from the server's handheld device to a display in the kitchen. By solving these very specific, high-pain problems, Toast was able to capture a massive share of the market, turning the humble cash register into the digital hub for the entire restaurant operation. They also created new revenue streams for themselves by acting as the payment processor, taking a small slice of every transaction that flowed through their system.

The vertical SaaS playbook was replicated across dozens of other complex industries. In construction, a sector notoriously slow to adopt technology, Procore Technologies built a multi-billion dollar empire. The company, founded in 2002 by a construction manager named Craig "Tooey" Courtemanche who was frustrated with the lack of effective software, created a unified platform to connect everyone on a job site—from the architect and general contractor to the subcontractors and the property owner. It became the single source of truth for project plans, financial data, and job site communications, replacing an archaic and error-prone system of spreadsheets, faxes, and overflowing binders. Procore succeeded because it was built by people who understood the grit and complexity of a real-world construction project.

The secret weapon for these vertical conquerors is almost always deep domain expertise. The founding team often consists of veterans from the industry they are targeting. This gives them an immediate and almost unfair advantage. They understand the nuances, the acronyms, and the unwritten rules of the industry. This credibility allows them to build trust with their first customers, who are often skeptical of outsiders. The software they build reflects this insider knowledge. The user interface uses familiar terminology, and the workflows are designed to mirror and improve upon the established processes of the industry, not force users to learn a completely new way of working.

Furthermore, many specialized industries are governed by a dense web of regulations and compliance requirements. For businesses in these fields, compliance is not an optional extra; it is a license to operate. Vertical SaaS providers turn this burden into a powerful selling point by building the necessary compliance checks and reporting features directly into their software. A healthcare SaaS will be designed from the ground up to be HIPAA compliant. A financial services platform will have features to help its customers meet the requirements of the SEC. This transforms the software from a simple productivity tool into an essential risk management solution.

While the Total Addressable Market (TAM) for any single vertical is, by definition, smaller than that of a horizontal product, the goal of the vertical player is to achieve a much higher level of market penetration. They don't need to sell to every business in the world; they just need to become the undisputed leader within their chosen niche. The ultimate ambition for many of these companies is to become the industry's central platform, expanding beyond pure software to offer a range of services. A vertical SaaS company that serves independent auto repair shops might start with shop management software, then add on payment processing, then create a marketplace for buying spare parts at a discount, and eventually even offer financing for new equipment.

Of course, the model is not without its risks. By tying their fortunes so closely to a single industry, vertical SaaS companies are exposed to that industry's cyclical downturns and disruptions. A platform built for the oil and gas exploration industry will suffer when oil prices plummet. Moreover, the horizontal giants have not stood still. Seeing the success of the vertical specialists, players like Salesforce have launched their own "industry clouds,"—pre-configured versions of their platform tailored for sectors like financial services, healthcare, and manufacturing. The primary defense for the pure-play vertical provider remains their superior depth of knowledge and the purpose-built nature of their product. They are not a horizontal platform wearing an industry-specific costume; they are a native of the industry, born and bred to solve its unique challenges. This authenticity is a powerful and difficult advantage to overcome.

CHAPTER ELEVEN: The Network Effect: How Cloud Platforms Create Moats

In the brutal, hyper-competitive world of software, a great product is not enough. A clever business model is not enough. Even a head start is not enough. The history of technology is littered with the corpses of superior products that were outmaneuvered and ultimately crushed by a competitor with a seemingly unassailable advantage. In the long run, the cloud empires that endure are not necessarily the ones with the best code or the most features, but the ones that have managed to construct the deepest and widest competitive moat around their business. This moat, a concept popularized by the investor Warren Buffett, is the structural advantage that protects a company from attack. And in the digital realm, the most powerful substance for building such a moat is the network effect.

The principle is deceptively simple: a product or service exhibits a network effect when it becomes more valuable as more people use it. The classic example is the telephone. A single telephone is a useless curiosity. Two telephones create a network of two. A million telephones create a network with nearly a trillion possible connections, making the device an indispensable part of modern life. This is often quantified by Metcalfe's Law, which states that the value of a telecommunications network is proportional to the square of the number of connected users. While the precise mathematics can be debated, the core insight is undeniable. In a networked world, value is not linear; it is exponential.

Cloud software, by its very nature of being connected and centralized, is a perfect breeding ground for these effects. Once a platform reaches a certain critical mass of users, a powerful flywheel begins to spin, attracting more users simply because of its existing user base. This creates a formidable barrier to entry for any potential rival. A new competitor cannot simply build a product with feature parity; they must somehow replicate the network that gives the incumbent its value. It is a classic chicken-

and-egg problem that has thwarted countless would-be challengers. The network effect is the invisible force that transforms a popular product into a locked-in standard.

The most straightforward manifestation of this principle is the direct network effect. This occurs when the value for any given user increases directly with the number of other users on the same network. This is the primary moat for the SaaS tools that have come to define modern collaboration and communication. A platform like Slack is a perfect case study. The first person in a company to sign up for Slack gets zero value from it; there is no one to talk to. The second person makes it minimally useful. But as the entire team, then the entire department, and finally the entire company adopts it, its value explodes. It becomes the company's central nervous system, the default place for every conversation, file share, and announcement.

At this point, the platform is no longer just a tool; it is a standard. An employee's proficiency in using Slack becomes a core job skill within that organization. The idea of switching to a new, competing chat application, even if it claims to be 10% faster or have a slicker interface, becomes almost unthinkable. The cost of such a migration would be measured not in dollars, but in the immense friction of retraining thousands of employees and the loss of years of archived conversational history. The network of users has created a powerful form of lock-in. The same dynamic applies to design collaboration tools like Figma, which transformed the solitary act of interface design into a real-time, multiplayer experience. The more designers and stakeholders within a company who use Figma, the more essential it becomes as the single source of truth for the company's products.

While direct network effects are powerful, especially within the walls of a single organization, an even more potent and expansive version is the indirect network effect, also known as a two-sided network effect. This is the engine that powers the true platform empires. In this model, the platform serves two distinct groups of users, and the value for one group increases as more users from the other group join. Think of a credit card: the card is more valuable to consumers if more merchants accept it, and it is more valuable to merchants if more consumers carry it. The platform in the middle—Visa or Mastercard—benefits from a virtuous cycle that reinforces its dominance on both sides.

In the SaaS world, the quintessential example of the two-sided network effect is the application marketplace. As we saw with Salesforce and the launch of its AppExchange, this was a strategic masterstroke that transformed a successful product into an entire economy. On one side of the platform are the Salesforce customers. On the other side are the thousands of independent software developers. As more customers adopted Salesforce, it became an increasingly attractive market for developers to build specialized applications for. As more high-quality applications appeared on the AppExchange—for everything from accounting to human resources—the core Salesforce platform became vastly more powerful and useful for its customers.

This creates a self-perpetuating cycle of immense power. A new CRM competitor entering the market is not just competing with Salesforce's core features; it is competing with Salesforce plus the thousands of apps in its ecosystem. For a customer to switch, they would have to find replacements for not just the CRM, but for all the specialized AppExchange tools they rely on to run their business. The developer community, in turn, has little incentive to build for the new platform because it lacks customers. This dynamic starves the challenger of both the customers and the ecosystem extensions needed to compete, creating an almost insurmountable moat for the incumbent.

Shopify replicated this playbook to perfection in the world of e-commerce. Its core product provides merchants with the tools to build and run an online store. But its true defensibility comes from its massive two-sided network. On one side are the millions of merchants who use the platform. On the other is a thriving ecosystem of app developers and theme designers. A merchant who needs a specialized feature, like a subscription billing tool or a customer loyalty program, can find dozens of options in the Shopify App Store. An entrepreneur who wants a unique look for their store can choose from thousands of professionally designed themes. This vast optionality makes the Shopify platform far more valuable than its core features alone would suggest. The developers and designers, in turn, are drawn to the platform because it gives them access to the largest possible market of potential customers. The two sides of the network feed each other, making Shopify's position as the operating system for e-commerce incredibly difficult to assail.

A third, more subtle but equally powerful network effect has emerged with the rise of artificial intelligence: the data network effect. As we explored in a previous chapter, SaaS platforms are in a unique position to collect massive amounts of aggregated, anonymized user data. This data is the fuel for training sophisticated machine learning models that can then deliver intelligent, predictive features back to the users. This creates its own powerful flywheel. A product with more users collects more data. This larger dataset allows it to train a smarter AI model. The smarter features make the product more effective and valuable, which in turn attracts more users, who generate even more data.

Consider a SaaS tool that helps businesses prevent customer churn. The more customer data the model can analyze—from thousands of different businesses—the better it gets at identifying the subtle warning signs that a customer is about to cancel their subscription. A new competitor might be able to copy the software's user interface, but it cannot copy the years of proprietary data that make the incumbent's predictive model so accurate. The intelligence of the product is itself a function of the network's scale. The product gets smarter as more people use it, creating a compelling reason for new customers to choose the market leader and a difficult-to-replicate advantage that grows stronger over time.

Finally, there is the integration network effect, which operates at the level of a company's entire software stack. In the modern enterprise, no application is an island. A typical company uses dozens of different SaaS tools, and the value of any single tool is greatly enhanced by its ability to connect to the others. This has led to certain platforms becoming the "system of record" or the gravitational center around which other applications orbit. Once a platform achieves this central status, its stickiness increases dramatically.

Salesforce, again, is a prime example. It is often the central repository for all customer data. As such, the marketing automation platform, the customer support platform, and the accounting platform all need to integrate with it. When a company is evaluating a new marketing tool, one of the first questions they will ask is, "How well does it integrate with Salesforce?" A tool with a deep, seamless integration has a huge advantage over one that does not. This forces the entire ecosystem of other SaaS vendors to prioritize building robust integrations with the market leader, which further entrenches the leader's central position. To rip out the central platform would mean breaking dozens of critical workflows and re-integrating the entire software stack around a new core. The switching cost becomes prohibitively high.

These different types of network effects rarely exist in isolation. The most dominant cloud platforms layer them on top of each other to create a multi-layered defense. Atlassian, for instance, benefits from a direct network effect for its Jira and Confluence products; the more people in an organization who use them, the more they become the standard for project tracking and documentation. It also benefits from a two-sided network effect through the Atlassian Marketplace, which offers thousands of third-party apps and plugins that extend the core functionality. And finally, it enjoys an integration network effect, as countless other development tools are built to integrate seamlessly with the Jira workflow.

Building a moat via network effects is not an accident; it is a deliberate and strategic process. It requires designing the product from day one to be not just a standalone tool, but a connected platform. It involves making the conscious decision to open up APIs, to encourage a developer ecosystem, and to build features that are inherently collaborative. It means understanding that in many markets, the initial goal is not profitability, but the rapid acquisition of a critical mass of users to kickstart the network flywheel.

Once that flywheel is spinning at full speed, it becomes a force of nature. The platform's growth becomes self-sustaining, and its position in the market becomes incredibly stable. The moat is no longer just a defensive structure; it becomes an offensive weapon. The network itself becomes the product's most compelling feature, a benefit that no upstart competitor can credibly claim to offer. This is how the most durable cloud empires are secured, not by building higher walls, but by creating an irresistible gravitational pull.

CHAPTER TWELVE: Collaboration and Communication: The New Work OS

For decades, the undisputed operating system of knowledge work was an unlikely pairing: the email inbox and the Microsoft Office file. This combination was so deeply entrenched, so universally accepted, that for many it was not a conscious choice but simply the digital air they breathed. Work was a relentless cycle of composing, sending, receiving, and forwarding messages. Progress was measured in the attachments sent back and forth, a clumsy digital ballet that created a trail of file versions with increasingly desperate names: `Quarterly_Report_v3.docx`, `Quarterly_Report_v3_Jens_edits.docx`, `Quarterly_Report_v4_FINAL.docx`, `Quarterly_Report_v4_FINAL_USE_THIS_ONE.docx`.

This workflow was a study in friction and fragmentation. The inbox was a black hole, a private silo where crucial information would disappear, accessible only to the sender and recipient. A new team member starting a project had no easy way to access the months of email conversations that had preceded their arrival. Locating the canonical, most up-to-date version of a document was a constant, low-grade scavenger hunt. Collaboration was a strictly sequential process: one person would work on a file, save it, and email it to the next person, who would then wait their turn. The idea of two people working on the same document at the same time was not just technically impossible; it was conceptually alien.

This clumsy reality was ripe for disruption. The first tremors of the earthquake came not from a direct assault on the document, but from an attack on the inbox's dominance as the center of all communication. While consumer chat applications like AIM and MSN Messenger had existed for years, they were seen as frivolous distractions in the corporate world. The enterprise needed something built for the unique rhythms of teamwork. The company that would ultimately crack this code and redefine workplace communication was a startup born from the ashes of a failed video game. The game was called Glitch; the internal tool its developers built to communicate with each other would become Slack.

Launched in 2013, Slack's proposition was to move team conversations out of private email inboxes and into persistent, organized, and searchable channels. This was a fundamental architectural shift in how information flowed within an organization. A channel dedicated to a specific project (#project-phoenix), a team (#marketing-team), or even a social interest (#dog-lovers) created a public square where all relevant parties could see the conversation unfold in real-time. A new person added to the channel could simply scroll up to read the entire history of the project, instantly getting up to speed. This transparency was revolutionary.

Slack's genius was rooted in its user experience, a masterclass in the design-centric philosophy that was coming to define the new wave of SaaS. The interface was clean, colorful, and infused with a playful personality. The sound design, the customizable loading messages, and the friendly "Slackbot" all contributed to an experience that felt less like a rigid corporate tool and more like a consumer application you actually wanted to use. This delight-focused design was a key driver of its bottom-up adoption. A single team could start using the free version, fall in love with it, and its use would spread organically through an organization until the IT department had little choice but to purchase the enterprise version.

Crucially, Slack was designed from the ground up to be a hub, not just another silo. It leveraged the API economy to build a vast ecosystem of integrations. A new commit in GitHub, a new support ticket in Zendesk, a new lead in Salesforce—all of these events could be piped as notifications directly into the relevant Slack channel. This transformed Slack from a simple chat application into a central command center, a single pane of glass through which a team could monitor the pulse of their entire operation. It was a direct challenge to the inbox as the primary notification layer of work.

While Slack was reinventing communication, another giant was methodically dismantling the tyranny of the file attachment. Google, with its suite of web-based applications, had been quietly building an alternative to Microsoft Office for years. The true revolution, however, was not just in making a word processor or a spreadsheet that ran in a browser; it was in completely changing the nature of the document itself. A Google Doc was not a static file; it was a living, web-based entity, accessed via a URL.

This simple architectural difference unlocked a new paradigm of collaboration. For the first time, multiple people could be inside the same document at the same time, their cursors blinking and moving as they typed, edited, and shaped the content together. The endless chain of email attachments was replaced by a single, definitive source of truth. Version control was no longer a user's responsibility; it was a built-in feature, with a complete revision history accessible with a click. The addition of commenting and suggestion features created a rich layer of conversation that lived directly alongside the work itself, providing context that was previously lost in sprawling email threads.

This real-time, simultaneous collaboration was a superpower. It accelerated the pace of work, collapsing a feedback cycle that used to take days into a matter of minutes. The Google Workspace (formerly G Suite) platform, which bundled Docs, Sheets, and Slides with Gmail and Google Drive, became the default operating system for a generation of startups and digitally native companies. It offered an elegant, cloud-first alternative to the on-premise, file-centric world of Microsoft, and its collaborative features were something the incumbent was slow to replicate effectively.

The third pillar of the new work OS to be rebuilt in the cloud was the meeting. For years, video conferencing was the exclusive domain of large corporations with the budget to install expensive, complex hardware systems from companies like Polycom or Cisco in dedicated boardrooms. These systems were notoriously difficult to use, often requiring IT support just to get a call started. For everyone else, meetings were either in-person or conducted over a crackly conference call line. The SaaS revolution changed this, making high-quality, face-to-face video communication a cheap and ubiquitous utility.

No company exemplified this shift more dramatically than Zoom. Founded in 2011 by a former lead engineer from Cisco's Webex, Zoom entered a crowded market with a singular focus: build a video conferencing service that was utterly simple and reliable. While competitors were adding feature after feature, Zoom obsessed over the core user experience. It made joining a meeting a one-click affair. It invested heavily in its underlying infrastructure to ensure that the video and audio quality remained stable, even on less-than-perfect internet connections. This relentless focus on "it just works" created a legion of loyal fans.

When the COVID-19 pandemic forced a sudden, global shift to remote work in 2020, Zoom was perfectly positioned. Its usage exploded on a scale almost unprecedented in the history of software, growing from 10 million daily meeting participants in December 2019 to over 300 million just four months later. The word "Zoom" became a verb, synonymous with the act of video calling, cementing its place as an essential component of the modern work toolkit.

With these three powerful, best-of-breed categories established— channel-based chat, real-time documents, and frictionless video— the stage was set for the next great battle: the fight for integration and control. A new, grander ambition emerged among these cloud players. It was no longer enough to be the best tool for a single job; the goal was to become the all-encompassing "Work Operating System," the single application where work begins and ends.

Microsoft, having seen its decades-long dominance of enterprise productivity threatened by these nimble cloud-native upstarts, was not going to go down without a fight. Under the cloud-first leadership of Satya Nadella, the company mounted a massive and incredibly effective counter-offensive. It did not try to beat Slack at its own game by building a standalone competitor. Instead, in 2017, it launched Microsoft Teams, a product that was deeply integrated into its existing Office 365 subscription, a service already used by hundreds of millions of people.

Teams was more than just a chat application. It was a unified hub that combined persistent chat, video meetings, and file storage with deep, native integrations into the Office applications that knowledge workers still spent most of their day in. From within a Teams channel, a user could co-author a Word document, update an Excel spreadsheet, or present a PowerPoint slide. This was a powerful bundling strategy. Microsoft's pitch to the CIO was simple: you are already paying for Office 365, and Teams is included. Why would you pay extra for Slack, Zoom, and Dropbox when you can get a tightly integrated solution from a single vendor you already trust? This strategy was brutally effective, leveraging Microsoft's colossal distribution advantage to rapidly propel Teams into a market-leading position.

As the giants of communication and productivity battled for supremacy, another category of software was making its own claim to be the central nervous system of work. These were the work management platforms, tools like Asana, Monday.com, Trello, and a flexible newcomer called Notion. These companies argued that the true center of work was not the conversation or the document, but the task and the project. Their platforms provided a structured environment for planning, tracking, and managing the work itself.

These tools evolved from simple to-do lists into highly visual and customizable platforms. They allowed teams to manage complex projects using a variety of methodologies, from simple Kanban boards to detailed Gantt charts. Like the communication hubs, they also became powerful platforms for integration, pulling in information from other tools to provide a holistic view of a project's status. Their pitch was that communication should happen in the context of the work. Instead of discussing a task in a noisy Slack channel, the conversation could happen directly on the task card itself, ensuring all context was preserved and easily findable.

Notion represented a particularly interesting evolution in this space, blending documents, databases, and project management tools into a single, flexible workspace. It gave users a set of powerful building blocks—text, tables, boards, calendars—and allowed them to construct their own customized workflows and operating systems. For many teams, Notion became a single destination for everything from project roadmaps and meeting notes to company wikis and employee directories, demonstrating a powerful trend toward consolidation and customizability.

By the early 2020s, the outlines of this new Work OS had become clear. It was not a single product from a single company, but a fluid, interconnected ecosystem of powerful SaaS tools. The average employee's digital workspace now consisted of a primary communication hub (like Slack or Teams), a collaborative productivity suite (Google Workspace or Microsoft 365), a ubiquitous video conferencing tool (Zoom), and a structured work management platform (like Asana or Jira).

The glue holding this all together was a web of seamless integrations, powered by the API economy. These connections created automated workflows that eliminated manual drudgery and kept information flowing. A "deal closed" alert from Salesforce in a Slack channel could automatically trigger the creation of a new project in Asana, which in turn would generate a new client folder in Google Drive. This level of automation and interoperability was the fulfillment of the cloud's early promise.

This radical transformation in the tools of work has had an equally radical impact on the nature of work itself. It is the technological foundation that has enabled the widespread adoption of remote and hybrid work models, allowing teams to collaborate effectively regardless of physical location. It has fostered a culture of greater transparency and real-time awareness. However, it has also introduced new challenges. The constant stream of notifications from these "always-on" platforms has blurred the lines between work and life, creating a very real risk of employee burnout. The digital workplace is more efficient and connected than ever before, but it is also more demanding, a firehose of information that requires new skills and cultural norms to manage effectively. The old operating system of email and attachments has been decisively replaced, and the new one, for all its power, is still evolving.

CHAPTER THIRTEEN: The Low-Code/No-Code Movement: Democratizing Software Creation

For most of its history, the act of creating software was a form of modern alchemy, a discipline shrouded in the complex syntax of programming languages and accessible only to a specialized priesthood of engineers. If a business needed a new tool—a custom application to manage inventory, a portal for customer feedback, or a unique workflow to track approvals—it had to petition this priestly class. The process was invariably slow, expensive, and often frustrating. A simple idea from the marketing department would be translated, often imperfectly, into a dense technical specification, which would then disappear into the IT department's cavernous project backlog, with an estimated delivery date somewhere in the next fiscal year. This chasm between the people with the business problems and the people with the coding skills was the single greatest bottleneck to innovation within most organizations.

The SaaS revolution had already lowered the barrier to *accessing* powerful software, but the barrier to *creating* it remained stubbornly high. The low-code/no-code movement emerged as a direct assault on this final barrier. It was founded on a simple, yet profoundly radical, premise: what if you didn't need to be a coder to build software? What if you could assemble an application visually, piece by piece, like building with digital LEGOs? This idea promised to do for software creation what the word processor did for document creation, transforming it from a specialized technical task into a mainstream business skill. It was the next logical step in the democratization of technology, placing the power to build not just in the hands of the few, but in the hands of the many.

The movement is best understood as a spectrum, with "no-code" at one end and "low-code" at the other. No-code platforms are the purest expression of this new philosophy. They are designed for the "citizen developer"—a term for a business user who understands their process intimately but has no formal training in programming. The interface is entirely visual, centered on a drag-and-drop editor. To build an application, a user pulls pre-built components from a palette onto a canvas, connects them, and defines their logic through simple, plain-English rules and dropdown menus. The goal is to abstract away every line of code, allowing the user to focus entirely on the "what" (the business outcome) rather than the "how" (the underlying technical implementation).

Low-code platforms occupy the middle ground. They are aimed at a more technical audience, including professional developers and the IT departments that support them. While they also rely heavily on visual development environments to accelerate the process, they provide an "escape hatch." When a developer hits a limitation in the visual builder—a need for a complex algorithm, a custom integration with a legacy system, or a highly specific user interface element—they can open a code editor and write custom JavaScript, Python, or SQL to extend the platform's capabilities. The mantra of low-code is not to replace developers, but to make them exponentially more productive, automating the tedious, repetitive 80% of the work so they can focus their expertise on the complex 20% that truly requires their skills.

This idea of visual, simplified programming was not entirely new. It had conceptual ancestors in the fourth-generation programming languages (4GLs) of the 1980s and in desktop database tools like Microsoft Access and FileMaker Pro, which allowed users to build simple applications for managing data. However, these early attempts were prisoners of the on-premise world. The applications they built were siloed on a single computer or a local network, were difficult to share, and couldn't easily connect to other systems. The modern low-code/no-code movement was born in the cloud, and this made all the difference. The cloud provided the universal accessibility, the API economy provided the connective tissue, and the SaaS business model provided the perfect delivery mechanism for these new creation platforms.

The pioneers of the no-code space often focused on solving a single, high-pain problem. In the world of web development, tools like Webflow and Bubble emerged as powerful alternatives to both simple, template-based site builders and complex, code-heavy frameworks. Webflow gave graphic designers the power to build sophisticated, responsive websites with complex animations and interactions, translating their visual designs directly into clean, production-ready code without them ever having to write it. Bubble went a step further, allowing entrepreneurs and creators to build fully functional, data-driven web applications, complete with user accounts, databases, and complex workflows. Suddenly, building a prototype for a new social network, an internal company directory, or a two-sided marketplace was something a single, non-technical founder could achieve in a matter of weeks, not months.

Another critical pillar of the no-code world was built around workflow automation. Platforms like Zapier and Integromat (later rebranded as Make) were not designed for building user-facing applications, but for creating the invisible plumbing that connects the modern software stack. They acted as a universal translator for the API economy. A business user could, with a few clicks, create an automated workflow—or "Zap"—that said, "When a customer submits a new entry on our Typeform survey, create a new row in our Airtable database, add the customer's email to our Mailchimp list, and post a notification in our #new-leads Slack channel." This ability to stitch together disparate SaaS tools into a single, automated process eliminated countless hours of mind-numbing manual data entry and empowered teams to design their own unique operational workflows.

At the heart of many of these custom applications and workflows was a new kind of tool that blurred the lines between a spreadsheet and a database. Airtable was the breakout star of this category. It presented users with a familiar, friendly, spreadsheet-like grid, but underneath this simple interface was a powerful relational database. Users could define different field types—text, numbers, attachments, checkboxes—and, crucially, link records between different tables. This allowed a marketing team, for example, to build a sophisticated content calendar that linked authors to articles, articles to social media campaigns, and campaigns to performance metrics. Airtable became the flexible, user-friendly backend for a huge swath of the no-code ecosystem, a place where citizen developers could structure and store their data without needing to understand the complexities of SQL.

While the no-code movement was empowering individual creators and small teams, the low-code movement was mounting a strategic offensive inside the world's largest companies. The primary target was the chronic and seemingly incurable ailment of the corporate IT department: the application backlog. In any large enterprise, the demand for new software solutions from business units vastly outstripped the central IT team's capacity to deliver them. Low-code platforms from vendors like OutSystems and Mendix, along with the offerings from established giants like Microsoft's Power Platform, offered a cure. They provided a sanctioned and governed environment where business units could build many of their own solutions.

This had a twofold benefit. First, it dramatically accelerated the pace of innovation. A department that needed a simple mobile app for its field sales team to check inventory no longer had to wait a year for the central IT team to build it. A small, cross-functional team, working with the low-code platform, could potentially build and deploy the app themselves in a matter of weeks. This freed business users from their dependence on overburdened developers and allowed them to solve their own problems with a speed that was previously unimaginable.

Second, it helped to solve the persistent problem of "shadow IT." For years, frustrated business users had resorted to using unapproved and often insecure tools—complex Excel macros, personal Dropbox accounts, or consumer-grade web apps—to get their jobs done. This created a massive blind spot for the IT department, full of security risks and data governance nightmares. Enterprise-grade low-code platforms brought this activity out of the shadows. They provided a secure, managed environment where citizen developers could build applications, but with central IT retaining control over data access, security policies, and deployment processes. It was a grand compromise: business units got the speed and autonomy they craved, and the IT department got the governance and control it required.

The ripple effects of this movement spread throughout the entire SaaS ecosystem. Recognizing the demand for greater customizability, many leading SaaS companies began embedding low-code and no-code capabilities directly into their own platforms. Salesforce had been a forerunner in this area for years with its suite of visual tools that allowed administrators to build custom objects, page layouts, and automated workflows without writing code. This trend accelerated, with project management platforms adding custom workflow builders and HR systems allowing users to design their own onboarding processes. This made the core SaaS products stickier and more powerful, allowing customers to tailor the software to their precise needs.

For the world of entrepreneurship, the impact was equally profound. The low-code/no-code movement dramatically lowered the cost and technical expertise required to launch a new software venture. An aspiring founder with deep industry knowledge but no coding ability could now build a fully functional minimum viable product (MVP) on their own. They could test their core assumptions, attract their first paying customers, and prove out their business model before ever needing to hire an expensive engineering team. It was the ultimate expression of the "Lean Startup" methodology, enabling a new wave of founders to bring their ideas to life.

Of course, this new paradigm was not a panacea. The abstractions that made no-code tools so easy to use also imposed limitations. An application built on a no-code platform might struggle with the performance and scalability required to serve millions of users. There was also the ever-present danger of the "cliff," the point at which the application's requirements would exceed the capabilities of the visual builder. A business might invest months in building a complex system on a no-code platform, only to discover it couldn't handle a single, mission-critical piece of custom logic, forcing a painful and expensive decision to scrap the project and start over with traditional code.

Furthermore, while the movement eliminated the need to write code, it did not eliminate the need to think like a software developer. Building a well-structured, secure, and user-friendly application still required a deep understanding of data modeling, process logic, and user experience design. The tools lowered the barrier to entry, but they did not eliminate the principles of good craftsmanship. A badly designed process, when automated, simply becomes a badly designed automated process. The potential for citizen developers to create a new kind of digital spaghetti, with convoluted workflows and poorly managed data, was very real. The democratization of creation also meant the democratization of the ability to create a mess.

CHAPTER FOURTEEN: Navigating the Regulatory Landscape: Compliance in a Global Cloud

In the heady, early days of the cloud, the internet felt like a new and lawless frontier. Data, freed from the confines of physical servers, flowed across international borders with the frictionless ease of an email. For the burgeoning SaaS empires, the world was a single, flat market. An application built in a Silicon Valley garage could be sold to a customer in Germany or Japan with little more than a credit card form. The physical location of the server on which the customer's data resided was a technical detail, a matter of latency and cost optimization, not of national sovereignty. This borderless ideal, however, was a temporary illusion. As the cloud grew from a niche for startups into the foundational infrastructure of the global economy, the world's governments and regulators inevitably began to take notice. The digital frontier was about to be carved up, mapped, and fenced.

The core of the issue was a fundamental conflict between the placeless nature of the cloud and the place-based nature of the law. A nation's laws apply within its borders, but where, precisely, is "the cloud"? Is it where the company is headquartered? Where the user is located? Or in the specific country where the physical server happens to be spinning? The answer, it turned out, was "all of the above," and the resulting complexity would transform the business of SaaS, turning legal compliance from a back-office chore into a primary strategic concern. The age of innocence was over; the age of the audit had begun.

This new reality was built on the concept of "data sovereignty," the idea that a nation's data is subject to the laws of the country in which it is located. Governments grew increasingly uneasy with the notion that their citizens' personal information, their corporations' intellectual property, and even their government's own sensitive data was being stored in massive, anonymous data centers on foreign soil, subject to the laws and surveillance capabilities of another country. This anxiety gave rise to a wave of data residency and data localization laws, regulations that mandated that certain types of data must be stored on physical servers located within a country's borders. For the SaaS industry, built on the efficiency of centralized, multi-tenant infrastructure, this was a direct challenge to its core architectural and economic model.

Long before the global privacy debate reached a fever pitch, the United States healthcare industry provided an early and potent case study in the power of industry-specific regulation. The Health Insurance Portability and Accountability Act (HIPAA), passed in 1996, set stringent national standards for the protection of sensitive patient health information. As healthcare providers began to move their operations to the cloud, any SaaS company wishing to serve this lucrative market had to contend with HIPAA's formidable requirements. This was not a simple matter of ticking a few boxes. It demanded a top-to-bottom re-engineering of the platform around security and privacy.

To be HIPAA compliant, a SaaS vendor had to implement a host of administrative, physical, and technical safeguards. This included everything from strict access controls and audit logs to employee training and encryption of all data, both in transit and at rest. Crucially, the vendor had to be willing to sign a "Business Associate Agreement" (BAA), a legally binding contract that made them directly liable for any breach of patient data, with potentially ruinous financial penalties. This immense liability filtered out the casual players, creating a market for specialized, vertical SaaS companies that could credibly claim to be a safe harbor for protected health information. The experience of adapting to HIPAA was a dress rehearsal for the even greater regulatory challenges to come.

The earthquake that truly shook the foundations of the global cloud industry struck on May 25, 2018. On that day, the European Union's General Data Protection Regulation (GDPR) came into effect. It was, and remains, the most comprehensive and stringent data privacy law in the world, and its impact was felt far beyond the borders of Europe. The law's most potent feature was its extraterritorial reach. It didn't matter where a company was based; if it processed the personal data of anyone residing in the EU, it had to comply with GDPR. Suddenly, a startup in Ohio or a marketing platform in Sydney was subject to the authority of European regulators.

GDPR was built on a set of powerful, individual-centric principles that fundamentally altered the relationship between businesses and the people whose data they held. It enshrined new rights for individuals, such as the "right to access" their data, the "right to data portability" (to take it with them to another service), and, most famously, the "right to be forgotten" (the right to have their personal data erased). The law mandated a new philosophy of "privacy by design" and "privacy by default," requiring companies to build data protection into their products from the very beginning, rather than treating it as an afterthought.

For SaaS companies, compliance was a monumental undertaking. They had to conduct detailed audits of every piece of personal data they collected, documenting what it was, why they were collecting it, and how long they were keeping it. User interfaces had to be redesigned to feature clear, unambiguous requests for consent, replacing the old model of pre-ticked boxes buried in lengthy terms of service. Many companies were required to appoint a Data Protection Officer (DPO) to oversee their compliance efforts. The stakes for getting it wrong were astronomical, with fines of up to 4% of a company's global annual revenue. GDPR effectively turned data privacy from a legal footnote into a C-suite priority and set a new, high-water mark for the rest of the world.

Inspired by GDPR's example, other jurisdictions began to follow suit. In the United States, which lacked a single federal privacy law, the state of California stepped into the void. The California Consumer Privacy Act (CCPA), which came into effect in 2020, granted Californians new rights over their data that were strikingly similar to those in GDPR. This was followed by the even stronger California Privacy Rights Act (CPRA). Soon, other states like

Virginia, Colorado, and Utah passed their own versions, creating a complex and costly patchwork of different state-level privacy regimes. For a SaaS company operating across the United States, compliance was no longer a matter of following a single set of rules, but of navigating a balkanized legal landscape where a user in Sacramento had different rights than a user in Salt Lake City.

The technical response from the cloud industry to this regulatory onslaught was swift and strategic. The IaaS giants—AWS, Azure, and Google Cloud—embarked on a massive global expansion, building data centers in dozens of countries. This was a direct answer to the challenge of data residency. A SaaS company could now choose to deploy its application in a specific "region"—such as Frankfurt, London, or Tokyo—and assure its customers that their data would never physically leave that jurisdiction. The cloud, paradoxically, re-materialized, its physical geography suddenly becoming a critical selling point. The ability to offer customers a choice of where their data would live became a standard feature and a crucial tool for navigating the new world of data sovereignty.

This new era of complexity also spawned its own ecosystem of solutions. A new category of "compliance-as-a-service" companies emerged. Firms like OneTrust and TrustArc built powerful SaaS platforms to help other companies manage their privacy programs, track data flows, and handle user consent. At the same time, companies like Vanta and Drata automated the painful and laborious process of preparing for security audits like SOC 2 and ISO 27001, turning a months-long consulting engagement into a streamlined, software-driven process. The cloud was now building the tools to regulate itself, creating a new and profitable market out of its own growing complexity.

Just as the industry was adapting to this new privacy-centric world, a deeper, more intractable conflict began to surface, pitting the national security interests of the United States against the privacy rights of the rest of the world. The heart of the conflict was the US Clarifying Lawful Overseas Use of Data Act, or CLOUD Act, passed in 2018. This law empowered US federal law enforcement to compel US-based technology companies to provide requested data, regardless of where on the planet that data was stored. An email from a German citizen stored on a Microsoft server in Dublin was, under this act, subject to a warrant from a court in Texas.

This assertion of authority placed US-based cloud providers in an impossible position. It was in direct and irreconcilable conflict with GDPR, which strictly forbids the transfer of EU citizens' data to a foreign country unless that country provides an "adequate" level of privacy protection. The European Court of Justice repeatedly ruled that the surveillance capabilities of the United States government meant that it did not, in fact, provide such adequate protection. In a landmark 2020 decision known as "Schrems II," the court invalidated the "Privacy Shield," the primary legal framework that thousands of companies used to transfer data between the EU and the US. The ruling threw the transatlantic data economy into a state of legal chaos, leaving cloud companies caught in a legal crossfire, forced to choose which superpower's laws they would violate.

This clash of legal titans highlighted a stark reality: the internet was no longer a single, global network. It was fracturing along geopolitical lines into a "Splinternet." The most extreme version of this was China, which had long operated its own digital ecosystem behind the "Great Firewall," requiring any foreign cloud provider to operate through a joint venture with a local Chinese company. But similar, if less overt, digital borders were being erected elsewhere, built not with firewalls but with regulations. Countries like Russia and India passed increasingly strict data localization laws, creating legal and technical hurdles for global SaaS providers.

For SaaS companies, this new regulatory landscape had profound business implications. On one hand, robust compliance became a powerful competitive advantage. The ability to produce a clean SOC 2 report or to demonstrate full GDPR compliance became a prerequisite for selling to any large enterprise. Sales cycles now routinely involved lengthy security questionnaires and legal reviews. A company that had invested in compliance could use it as a mark of trustworthiness and professionalism, a way to differentiate itself from less mature competitors.

On the other hand, the cost of compliance became a significant burden, especially for startups and smaller companies. Navigating the global maze of regulations required expensive legal advice and significant engineering effort. This created another structural advantage for the large, incumbent players who had the resources to maintain dedicated compliance teams and legal departments. In the end, the regulatory landscape became another force of gravity in the cloud ecosystem, pulling companies into the orbits of the major IaaS providers who could offer the global footprint and the certified infrastructure needed to operate in this complex new world. The dream of a borderless digital frontier had given way to a new reality: a global patchwork of digital jurisdictions, each with its own rules, its own risks, and its own gatekeepers.

CHAPTER FIFTEEN: The Venture Capital Fuel: Funding the Cloud Empires

The new architecture of the cloud was elegant, and the subscription business model was a work of commercial genius. But together, they created a peculiar and dangerous financial paradox. In the old on-premise world, a software sale was a tidal wave of cash. A multi-million dollar license fee would arrive in one glorious lump sum, covering the cost of the sale and generating a handsome profit all at once. The SaaS model, by contrast, was a slow, deliberate drip. A customer, acquired at a significant upfront cost, would only begin to pay back that investment in tiny monthly increments. This created a deep and perilous cash flow trough known as the "SaaS valley of death."

A new SaaS company could be wildly successful, signing up hundreds of new customers a month, and still be hurtling toward bankruptcy. Every new customer represented a net cash outflow. The company had to pay the salesperson's commission, the marketing campaign costs, and the onboarding specialists' salaries immediately. The revenue, however, would trickle in over the next twelve, twenty-four, or thirty-six months. To grow was to bleed cash. For the SaaS revolution to get off the ground, it needed a new kind of fuel, a financial engine capable of bridging this valley. That engine was venture capital.

The relationship between venture capital and Software as a Service was not one of instant attraction. In the early 2000s, most venture capitalists were conditioned to love the lumpy, predictable-in-its-unpredictability revenue of the perpetual license model. They understood big game hunting: find a massive deal, close it, and see the cash hit the bank account. The SaaS model, with its small initial payments and its focus on companies that were often deeply unprofitable on paper, looked strange and risky. It required a complete rewiring of the investor mindset, a shift from analyzing a single transaction to understanding the long-term economics of a relationship.

The key that unlocked this new understanding was a new set of metrics, a new language that allowed founders and investors to accurately model the future of a subscription business. This financial lexicon became the bedrock of every SaaS funding pitch. Foremost among these was Annual Recurring Revenue, or ARR. ARR was the north star, the single number that represented the baseline revenue a company could expect over the next twelve months if it didn't sign a single new customer or lose any existing ones. It was a measure of momentum and stability that the lumpy world of on-premise software could never provide. Investors could track its growth month-over-month, giving them a clear, real-time indicator of the company's trajectory.

If ARR was the measure of scale, the true health of the business was revealed by the delicate dance between two other acronyms: LTV and CAC. Customer Acquisition Cost (CAC) was the total bill for winning a new customer, encompassing all sales and marketing expenses. Customer Lifetime Value (LTV) was the total profit a company could expect to earn from that customer before they cancelled their subscription, a calculation that was intrinsically tied to the churn rate. This was the magic formula. As long as the LTV was significantly higher than the CAC—a ratio of 3:1 was often seen as the gold standard—the business had a license to print money.

This LTV-to-CAC ratio was the Rosetta Stone that allowed VCs to look at a company that was losing millions of dollars and see a future corporate giant. The losses weren't a sign of failure; they were a deliberate investment in future profits. Every dollar spent on sales and marketing was not an expense in the traditional sense, but the purchase of a future revenue stream. This insight turned the entire venture capital world on its head. The goal was no longer to achieve profitability as quickly as possible. The new game was to grow as fast as humanly, and financially, possible, pouring every available dollar into acquiring customers with positive unit economics.

This gave rise to the "growth at all costs" era of SaaS investing. The market was a massive land grab, and the company that could plant its flag on the most territory the fastest would win. The network effects and high switching costs inherent in many SaaS markets meant that the winner would likely take all, or at least most, of the prize. Being the second-best CRM or the third-most-popular project management tool was a recipe for mediocrity. Venture capitalists, recognizing this dynamic, were more than happy to fund years of losses in exchange for market leadership. The mandate from the board of directors to the CEO was simple and relentless: grow.

This insatiable appetite for growth was fueled by a procession of ever-larger funding rounds, each with its own letter of the alphabet. A "Seed" round would provide the initial capital to build a product and find the first few customers. A "Series A" round, typically raised once the company had found product-market fit and reached a milestone like $1 million in ARR, would fund the hiring of the first dedicated sales and marketing team. The "Series B" was for scaling, for pouring gasoline on the fire and proving the go-to-market playbook could be replicated on a massive scale. Subsequent rounds—C, D, E, and beyond—were for global expansion, strategic acquisitions, and cementing market dominance.

With each round, the valuations soared. In the absence of profits, investors settled on a new shorthand for valuing these companies: the ARR multiple. A fast-growing SaaS company could command a valuation that was ten, twenty, or, in the frothiest of times, even fifty times its current annual recurring revenue. A company with $10 million in ARR could suddenly be worth half a billion dollars. This new math led to an explosion in the population of "unicorns," privately held companies valued at over one billion dollars. The title became a badge of honor, a signal to the market that a company was a future titan in the making.

This influx of capital was not just a blank check. It came with a very specific set of expectations and a well-worn playbook, often codified and evangelized by a new generation of SaaS-focused venture capital firms. Firms like Bessemer Venture Partners became the high priests of the cloud economy, publishing influential "laws" and benchmarks for SaaS businesses. Andreessen Horowitz brought a new level of operational support, offering its portfolio companies access to a deep bench of experts in recruiting, marketing, and sales. Sequoia Capital continued its legendary run of picking winners, applying its decades of pattern recognition to this new model.

These firms did more than just provide money; they provided a roadmap. Having seen the journey from zero to IPO a dozen times over, they could offer invaluable advice on everything from pricing strategies and building a sales team to international expansion and preparing for a public offering. They sat on the boards of their portfolio companies, pushing them to hit aggressive growth targets and holding them accountable to the metrics that mattered. Their involvement was a powerful signaling mechanism; a company backed by a top-tier VC firm gained instant credibility, making it easier to attract talent and land those crucial first enterprise customers.

The vast majority of this venture capital firehose was aimed at two specific departments: product development (R&D) and, most significantly, sales and marketing. The money was used to hire legions of software engineers to build out new features and stay ahead of the competition. But even more was spent on armies of Sales Development Representatives (SDRs) to make cold calls, Account Executives (AEs) to close deals, and marketing teams to run vast digital advertising campaigns. The CAC was a ravenous beast, and the venture capital was its food.

The goal of this entire high-stakes enterprise was a massive "exit." For the venture capital model to work, every investment had to have the potential to return ten, twenty, or even one hundred times the initial capital, because for every runaway success like Salesforce, there were a dozen failures that would return nothing. The two primary paths to such an exit were a strategic acquisition by a larger company—like Google buying Looker or Salesforce buying MuleSoft—or the ultimate prize, an Initial Public Offering (IPO). An IPO was the moment a company graduated from the private markets to the public, offering its shares on a stock exchange and providing the liquidity that early investors and employees had been working toward for years.

This pressure-cooker environment, fueled by billions in venture capital, created a unique and often brutal corporate culture. The pace was relentless. The focus on quarterly growth targets was obsessive. The mantra was "up and to the right." While this environment produced incredible innovation and created immense wealth for many, it also led to burnout and a culture where growth was sometimes pursued at the expense of all else. The demands of the venture capital model meant that building a nice, stable, profitable "lifestyle" business was never an option. The only acceptable outcomes were world domination or a spectacular flameout.

For a time, it seemed the river of capital would flow forever and the ARR multiples would only ever increase. But the laws of financial gravity can only be suspended for so long. A series of market corrections and a global economic slowdown in the early 2020s brought a new, colder reality. Public market investors, spooked by rising interest rates, suddenly started caring about old-fashioned concepts like profitability. The sky-high valuations of many publicly traded cloud companies came crashing back to earth, and the shockwave was felt throughout the private venture capital markets.

The mantra in Silicon Valley boardrooms began to shift. "Growth at all costs" was quietly replaced by a new buzzword: "capital efficiency." The question was no longer simply "How fast can you grow?" but "How much does it cost you to grow?" Investors started looking for a path to profitability, not in a distant, hypothetical future, but on a clear and foreseeable timeline. A new benchmark gained prominence: the "Rule of 40." This rule of thumb stated that a healthy SaaS company's annual revenue growth rate plus its profit margin should equal or exceed 40%. A company growing at 60% could afford to have a -20% profit margin. A company growing at 20% needed to have a 20% profit margin to be considered in the same league.

This new focus on sustainable growth did not mean the end of venture capital's love affair with SaaS. The model's fundamental strengths—the predictable recurring revenue, the high gross margins, the sticky customer relationships—remained as attractive as ever. But the era of unlimited, no-questions-asked funding for growth at any price was over. It marked a maturation of the industry, a recognition that the ultimate goal was not just to build a unicorn, but to build an enduring, profitable, and self-sustaining business. The venture capital that had once been a rocket booster for the initial land grab had now become the long-term investment capital needed to build lasting empires.

CHAPTER SIXTEEN: The Go-To-Market Playbook: Marketing and Selling SaaS

The new world of cloud software demanded a new kind of salesperson. The old guard, the legendary "elephant hunters" of the on-premise era, were masters of a specific and arduous art. Their craft was one of steak dinners, golf courses, and year-long sales cycles, culminating in a seven-figure deal signed in a mahogany-paneled boardroom. They sold software the way one sells a corporate jet: a massive, one-time capital expenditure requiring layers of executive approval. This entire ritual, however, was spectacularly ill-suited to the reality of Software as a Service. You do not dispatch a team of bespoke suit-clad hunters to sell a fifty-dollar-a-month subscription. The economics were nonsensical.

The SaaS business model, with its low initial price points and its emphasis on volume and velocity, required a complete reinvention of the sales and marketing machine. The product was no longer a monolithic beast to be installed; it was a nimble service to be adopted. The customer relationship was not a single transaction; it was a continuous journey. This new reality gave birth to a new go-to-market playbook, a highly structured, data-driven, and ruthlessly efficient system for attracting, converting, and retaining customers at scale. It was less of an art and more of a science, an intricate assembly line designed to turn strangers into subscribers.

At the heart of this transformation was a fundamental shift in the sales floor itself. The expensive, travel-heavy field sales model, where account executives spent their days flying around the country, was largely replaced by a far more efficient engine: inside sales. The new SaaS salesperson was not based in the field but in the office, armed not with an expense account but with a headset and a suite of powerful digital tools. The Customer Relationship Management (CRM) system was their universe, a centralized brain for tracking every lead, contact, and interaction. Voice over IP (VoIP) phones and web conferencing tools like GoToMeeting and later Zoom became their meeting rooms, allowing them to conduct compelling product demonstrations for prospects anywhere in the world without ever leaving their desks.

This new model was an order of magnitude cheaper and more scalable. A single inside sales rep could manage a far larger pipeline of smaller deals than a traditional field rep, making the unit economics of a subscription business viable. The sales floor transformed into a high-energy, data-rich environment, often resembling the trading floor of an investment bank. Dashboards on large screens displayed real-time metrics: calls made, demos booked, deals closed. The sales process itself was broken down into a series of predictable, measurable stages, allowing for constant optimization and forecasting with a level of accuracy the old world could only dream of.

Of course, for this high-velocity sales engine to run, it needed a constant supply of high-quality fuel. The old marketing playbook of cold calling, trade show booths, and glossy magazine ads was too expensive and too imprecise for this new world. The solution was a revolutionary approach that flipped the entire marketing paradigm on its head. Instead of "outbound" marketing that rudely interrupted potential customers, the new strategy was "inbound." The core philosophy was simple: instead of hunting for customers, make them come to you. The way to do this was to stop selling and start helping.

This gave rise to the content marketing machine. SaaS companies transformed their marketing departments into miniature publishing houses, churning out a steady stream of valuable, educational content designed to attract their ideal customer. The weapon of choice was the company blog, which became a platform for writing articles that directly addressed the pain points and questions of their target audience. A company selling accounting software wouldn't write about its features; it would write articles like "7 Common Invoicing Mistakes That Cost Small Businesses Money" or "A Founder's Guide to Understanding Cash Flow." The goal was to be the top result when a potential customer typed their problem into a Google search bar.

This strategy was built on the foundation of Search Engine Optimization (SEO). By creating high-quality content centered around the keywords their customers were using, SaaS marketers could capture a steady stream of organic, "free" traffic from search engines. This traffic was then directed toward the next stage of the process: lead capture. This was achieved through "gated" content, more substantial resources like white papers, ebooks, or recorded webinars that a visitor could access in exchange for their email address and a few other details. Just like that, an anonymous website visitor was converted into a known lead.

With this new influx of leads, a new challenge emerged: how to sort the merely curious from the genuinely interested. Bombarding the sales team with every single person who downloaded an ebook would be a colossal waste of their time. The solution was the creation of a structured, automated funnel, powered by a new category of SaaS known as marketing automation platforms. Companies like HubSpot, Marketo, and Pardot built the software that became the central nervous system for this entire inbound methodology.

This funnel had clearly defined stages. At the "Top of the Funnel" (TOFU), the goal was awareness, attracting visitors with blog posts and social media. Once a visitor provided their contact information, they became a "Marketing Qualified Lead" (MQL) and entered the "Middle of the Funnel" (MOFU). At this stage, the marketing automation platform would begin a process of "lead nurturing," sending the prospect a series of automated but personalized emails with more helpful content, gently guiding them toward a purchasing decision.

The system would also perform "lead scoring," assigning points to a lead based on their characteristics (like company size or job title) and their actions (visiting the pricing page, attending a webinar). Once a lead's score crossed a certain threshold, they were deemed ready to talk to a human and were automatically passed to the sales team as a "Sales Qualified Lead" (SQL). This automated triage system ensured that the expensive, highly trained sales reps spent their time only on the warmest, most promising prospects, dramatically increasing their efficiency and close rates.

To handle this structured flow of leads, the sales organization itself became highly specialized, breaking down the monolithic role of "salesperson" into a series of distinct, focused functions. This created a clear and efficient assembly line for converting leads into revenue.

The first role in this chain was the Sales Development Representative, or SDR (sometimes called a Business Development Representative, or BDR). The SDR's sole job was to qualify leads. They were the first human point of contact, responsible for responding to inbound SQLs and also for conducting targeted outbound prospecting to create new opportunities. Their mission was not to close deals, but to determine if a prospect had a genuine need, the budget to buy, and the authority to make a decision. If a prospect met these criteria, the SDR would book a product demonstration and hand them off to the next specialist in the line.

That specialist was the Account Executive, or AE. The AE was the closer. Their job was to take the qualified opportunities from the SDRs, conduct the product demonstrations, navigate the procurement process, and get the contract signed. By focusing exclusively on this "bottom of the funnel" activity, AEs could become masters of their craft, honing their demo skills and their ability to articulate the product's value proposition.

Once the deal was closed, the customer was passed to the final specialist in the traditional go-to-market chain: the Customer Success Manager, or CSM. As we will explore in the next chapter, the CSM's role was to be the "farmer," responsible for ensuring the customer was successfully onboarded, achieving their desired outcomes, and, ultimately, renewing and expanding their subscription over time.

Just as this sales-led model was being perfected and scaled across the industry, a new and even more disruptive go-to-market strategy began to emerge, one that threatened to make the traditional sales team obsolete for a large segment of the market. This was Product-Led Growth, or PLG. The PLG playbook, championed by a new generation of SaaS companies like Slack, Dropbox, and Atlassian, was built on a radical idea: the product itself should be the primary driver of customer acquisition, conversion, and expansion.

Instead of using content to generate a lead that a salesperson would then try to convert, the PLG model used the product itself as the top of the funnel. This was accomplished through a "freemium" or "free trial" offering. A user could sign up and start using a core version of the product instantly, without ever having to talk to a human being. The onboarding process was automated, designed to guide the user to their "aha!" moment as quickly as possible. The marketing and sales effort was focused not on selling a vision, but on getting a user to experience the product's value firsthand.

This created a powerful, bottom-up adoption model. An individual employee would discover a tool like Trello, start using the free version to manage their own tasks, and find it incredibly useful. They would then invite their immediate team members to collaborate. As the team's usage grew, they would eventually hit a usage limit or need a premium feature, prompting one of them to upgrade to a paid plan by simply entering a credit card. This viral, user-driven adoption could spread throughout an entire organization, often without the IT department or senior management even being aware of it until hundreds of employees were already using the tool.

This model gave rise to a new and more powerful type of lead: the "Product Qualified Lead," or PQL. A PQL was a user of the free product who had demonstrated strong buying signals through their actions *inside* the application. They might have repeatedly hit the paywall for a premium feature, invited their entire team, or imported a large amount of data. These signals were a far more accurate predictor of purchasing intent than any lead score from a marketing automation system. The sales team in a PLG company was not focused on chasing MQLs, but on engaging with PQLs, reaching out to help these highly engaged free users make the case for a company-wide enterprise plan.

This new world of SaaS also turned pricing and packaging into a critical strategic lever in the go-to-market playbook. The pricing page was no longer a static list of numbers; it was a core part of the customer acquisition and expansion strategy. The classic "per-seat" model was simple and predictable, but companies quickly adopted more sophisticated approaches. Tiered pricing—offering packages like "Basic," "Pro," and "Enterprise"—became the standard. This allowed a company to cater to different customer segments, from small businesses to large corporations, and it created a clear and compelling upsell path for customers as their needs grew.

An even more sophisticated model that gained traction was usage-based pricing. This was the philosophy of API-first companies like Twilio, which charged per text message sent, and data warehouse platforms like Snowflake, which charged for compute time and storage used. This model had the powerful advantage of perfectly aligning the customer's cost with the value they received. It also made initial adoption incredibly easy; a customer could start with a very small amount of usage and only pay more as their business grew and their reliance on the service increased. The pricing model itself became an engine for expansion.

While the direct-to-customer model, whether sales-led or product-led, defined the first decade of SaaS, a final piece of the go-to-market puzzle began to fall into place as the industry matured: the channel. To sell to the largest and most complex enterprise customers, and to expand into new international markets, SaaS companies began to build out partner ecosystems. These included value-added resellers (VARs) who would bundle the SaaS product with their own services, and system integrators (SIs) like Accenture or Deloitte who would implement the software as part of a larger digital transformation project for a Fortune 500 client. These partnerships provided the scale, local presence, and deep industry expertise that was often necessary to crack the most lucrative segments of the market. The playbook was complete, a multi-faceted and ever-evolving machine that had mastered the science of selling invisibility.

CHAPTER SEVENTEEN: Customer Success: The Key to Retention and Growth

The traditional sales process has a definitive and triumphant climax: the signature on the contract. In the on-premise world, this was the moment the champagne was uncorked. The deal was done, the revenue was booked, and the salesperson moved on to the next hunt. The customer was then handed off to a separate, and often disconnected, department known as "customer support" or "account management." The role of this department was largely reactive. They were the firefighters, the people you called when the software was broken, the server was down, or you couldn't find a feature. Their job was to fix problems and, once a year, to place a polite call to ensure the maintenance contract was renewed. The relationship was transactional, and the vendor's primary financial incentive ended the moment the initial sale was made.

The subscription economy rendered this entire model obsolete, and dangerously so. In a world where a customer could cancel their service with thirty days' notice, the signing of the contract was not the finish line; it was the starting gun. The old model of reactive support was a recipe for disaster in this new paradigm. A customer who only heard from their vendor when something was broken was a customer who was constantly being reminded of the software's failings, not its value. When the renewal date appeared on the horizon, their primary memory of the relationship would be a series of frustrating support tickets. This was a direct path to the single greatest existential threat to any SaaS business: churn.

Churn, the rate at which customers cancel their subscriptions, is the silent killer of the cloud. It is a leak in the revenue bucket that, if left unchecked, can make sustainable growth impossible. No matter how effective a company's sales and marketing engine is at pouring new customers into the top of the funnel, a high churn rate will ensure the bucket never fills. This reality forced the SaaS industry to invent an entirely new corporate function, a discipline built not on fixing what was broken, but on ensuring the customer never felt broken in the first place. This was the birth of Customer Success.

The core philosophy of Customer Success is a radical departure from the old world. It is founded on a simple, yet profound, conviction: the vendor is only successful if the customer is successful. It is a proactive, data-driven, and strategic discipline designed to ensure that customers achieve their desired outcomes while using the product. A Customer Success Manager, or CSM, is not a firefighter; they are a combination of architect, personal trainer, and strategic advisor. Their job begins the moment the sale is complete, and their primary mission is to shepherd the customer from their initial purchase to a state of deep, quantifiable value.

This journey begins with the single most critical phase in the customer lifecycle: onboarding. The first ninety days of a new customer's experience are a powerful predictor of their long-term loyalty. A clumsy, confusing, or unsupported onboarding process is a leading cause of early churn. The CSM's first task is to act as a sherpa, guiding the new customer from the base of the mountain to their first summit. This involves a structured process, not just a welcome email. It includes a formal kickoff call to understand the customer's specific business goals, a technical setup process to integrate the software into their existing stack, and a series of training sessions to ensure the end-users are comfortable and competent.

The primary goal of onboarding is to minimize the "Time to First Value" (TTV). This is the time it takes for a customer to experience the initial "aha!" moment, the point at which they see a tangible return on their investment and their decision to buy the software is validated. For a marketing automation platform, this might be the moment they successfully launch their first email campaign. For a project management tool, it might be the completion of their first project. The CSM's job is to accelerate this process, clearing any technical or educational hurdles that stand in the way and ensuring the customer gets an early win that builds momentum and confidence.

Once a customer is successfully onboarded, the focus of the CSM shifts from implementation to adoption. It is not enough for a customer to simply have access to the software; they must be actively and deeply using it. This is where the data-driven nature of the discipline comes into sharp focus. Modern Customer Success is not based on guesswork. It is powered by a constant stream of product usage data. A new generation of specialized Customer Success platforms, pioneered by companies like Gainsight, emerged to provide CSMs with a 360-degree view of their customers' health.

These platforms ingest data from a variety of sources: how often a user logs in, which features they are using, which features they are ignoring, the number of support tickets they have filed, and even their responses to satisfaction surveys. This data is then rolled up into a single, algorithmically generated "customer health score," typically represented as a simple red, yellow, or green indicator. This score acts as an early warning system. A customer whose usage has suddenly dropped off, or who has never adopted a key feature they are paying for, will see their health score turn yellow or red. This is a powerful, proactive trigger. Instead of waiting for the customer to call and complain or, worse, to simply cancel their subscription, the CSM is automatically alerted to the risk. They can then reach out with a helpful email, a "pro tip" on how to use a specific feature, or an offer for a targeted training session.

This proactive engagement is designed to move the customer up the value chain. The CSM is constantly looking for ways to help the customer get more out of the product. This could involve sharing best practices from other successful customers in the same industry or introducing them to new features they may not be aware of. This process of continuous value delivery is the most effective antidote to churn. A customer who sees their software vendor as a proactive partner invested in their success is far less likely to be swayed by a competitor's sales pitch. The relationship evolves from a simple vendor-customer dynamic to one of a trusted advisor.

However, the true strategic power of Customer Success lies in its transformation from a defensive, churn-fighting function into a powerful offensive engine for revenue growth. In the subscription economy, the initial sale is just the beginning of the revenue story. The largest and most successful SaaS companies do not just make money from new customers; they generate a huge portion of their growth from their existing customer base. This is where Customer Success becomes a critical partner to the sales organization.

Because the CSM has the deepest relationship with the customer and the clearest view into their day-to-day business, they are in the perfect position to identify opportunities for expansion. This is the commercial side of the CSM role. As they work with a customer, a CSM might notice that one department is having great success with the product. This is a natural trigger to suggest expanding the use of the software to other departments within the company. This is known as an "upsell." Alternatively, a CSM might recognize that a customer is struggling with a problem that could be solved by another product in the vendor's portfolio. This is a "cross-sell."

This focus on existing customer revenue gave rise to one of the most important metrics in the SaaS industry: Net Revenue Retention, or NRR (sometimes called Net Dollar Retention). NRR calculates what percentage of revenue from a cohort of customers a company has retained over a period, typically a year. It starts with 100% of the initial revenue and then subtracts any revenue lost to churn or downgrades, and adds any new revenue gained from upsells and cross-sells.

The holy grail for a SaaS business is an NRR of over 100%. An NRR of 120%, for example, means that for every dollar of revenue the company had at the beginning of the year, it now has $1.20, even *after* accounting for churn. This means the growth from the existing customer base is so strong that the company would continue to grow even if it failed to sign a single new customer. Public market investors came to see NRR as a primary indicator of a healthy, sticky, and efficient business model. Companies with best-in-class NRR, like Snowflake and Twilio, were rewarded with premium valuations. Achieving this level of retention and growth is virtually impossible without a world-class Customer Success organization.

Of course, providing this level of proactive, strategic engagement to every single customer is not economically feasible. A company with thousands of small business customers cannot afford to assign a dedicated CSM to each one. This reality forced the discipline to evolve and segment its approach, creating a tiered model for delivering success.

At the top of the pyramid is the "high-touch" model, reserved for the largest and most valuable enterprise accounts. These customers are assigned a dedicated CSM who acts as a true strategic partner, holding regular meetings, conducting quarterly business reviews (QBRs) to demonstrate ROI, and building deep relationships across the customer's organization.

In the middle is the "low-touch" or "tech-touch" model, designed for a larger volume of mid-market customers. Here, a single CSM might manage a portfolio of dozens or even hundreds of accounts. Their engagement is a blend of personal interaction and technology-driven outreach. They might host webinars for multiple clients at once or rely on automated, triggered email campaigns to deliver advice and best practices.

At the base of the pyramid is the "digital-led" model for the long tail of small business customers. Here, the entire customer success experience is delivered through technology. The onboarding is a series of self-guided, in-app tutorials. Proactive advice is delivered through automated emails and a comprehensive online knowledge base. Support is provided through a community forum where users can help each other. The goal is to provide the resources for customers to be successful on their own, at scale.

This segmentation and the increasing reliance on technology have turned Customer Success into a deeply data-driven science. The most sophisticated organizations no longer think of their customer relationships as a series of ad-hoc interactions. They see it as a "customer journey," a meticulously mapped and managed lifecycle with specific playbooks and automated interventions for every stage.

The organizational impact of this new function has been profound. In the early days, Customer Success was often a small team tucked away inside the sales or support department. But as its strategic importance became undeniable, it has been elevated to a C-level function in many of the most forward-thinking companies. The rise of the Chief Customer Officer (CCO) is a clear signal that the post-sale customer experience is now seen as being just as critical to the health of the business as sales or product development.

This has also forced a new level of internal collaboration. For Customer Success to be effective, it cannot operate in a silo. The CSM acts as the voice of the customer inside the company. They must feed insights about product gaps and feature requests back to the product team. They must collaborate with the marketing team to turn their happiest customers into advocates, case studies, and testimonials. And they must work hand-in-hand with the sales team to manage renewals and identify expansion opportunities. They are the connective tissue that binds the entire organization together around the shared goal of delivering value to the customer.

In the end, the invention of Customer Success was an inevitable consequence of the subscription model. It is the operational manifestation of a world where relationships have replaced transactions. It recognizes that the most valuable asset a cloud company possesses is not its code or its servers, but the loyalty of its customer base. In the empire of the cloud, where the next competitor is always just a click away, the surest path to long-term dominance is not just to acquire customers, but to make them so successful that they would never dream of leaving.

CHAPTER EIGHTEEN: The Culture of Innovation: Building and Scaling SaaS Teams

The software that came in a box was built by people who thought in boxes. The process was linear, sequential, and orderly, a series of discrete stages that flowed into one another like a slow-moving river. A team of business analysts would spend months gathering requirements, which were then solidified into a monolithic specification document. This document, the sacred text, was handed over the wall to the architects and developers, who would disappear for a year or more to build the product. After them, another team, the quality assurance testers, would spend months trying to break it. Finally, the finished artifact, frozen in time on a CD-ROM, would be shrink-wrapped and shipped. This was the "waterfall" model of development, and for the on-premise world, it made a certain kind of sense. When you only have one shot to get it right, you measure a dozen times before you cut.

The cloud shattered this model completely. A SaaS application is not a finished artifact; it is a living, breathing organism, a service that is never "done." It is in a perpetual state of becoming, with new code being deployed not once a year, but multiple times a day. This fundamental shift from a static product to a dynamic service demanded a radical reinvention of the teams that built it. The rigid, siloed departments of the waterfall era were replaced by something more fluid, more collaborative, and orders of magnitude faster. Building a cloud empire required a new kind of culture, an operating system for people that was as scalable and as agile as the software they were creating.

At the core of this cultural revolution were two interconnected philosophies that became the standard for virtually every successful SaaS company: Agile development and DevOps. Agile was a direct rebellion against the ponderous, document-heavy waterfall process. Instead of one massive, multi-year project, Agile broke the work down into a series of short, iterative cycles called "sprints," typically lasting one to four weeks. At the start of each sprint, a small, cross-functional team would pull a chunk of work from a prioritized backlog and commit to delivering a small, demonstrable piece of working software by the end of the cycle. This created a rapid and continuous feedback loop. The product was no longer a secret until the grand unveiling; it was evolving in plain sight, with constant opportunities for stakeholders to see the progress and adjust the priorities based on real-world learning.

If Agile was the "what" and the "when" of this new process, DevOps was the "how." The term, a portmanteau of "Development" and "Operations," represented a profound cultural and technical shift. In the old world, developers and the operations teams who managed the servers were two separate kingdoms, often with conflicting goals. Developers wanted to ship new features as fast as possible. Operations, or "Ops," wanted to maintain stability, and every new change was a potential threat to that stability. This created a natural friction, a "wall of confusion" that slowed everything down. DevOps sought to tear down that wall. It was a movement built on shared responsibility, automation, and the idea that the people who build the software should also be responsible for running it in production.

This new partnership was enabled by a powerful set of engineering practices. The most important of these was the creation of the Continuous Integration and Continuous Deployment (CI/CD) pipeline. This was an automated assembly line for code. When a developer finished a piece of work, they would check their code into a shared repository. This action would automatically trigger a series of events: the system would build the software, run a battery of automated tests to check for bugs and regressions, and, if all the tests passed, deploy the new code directly to the live production environment, often without any human intervention. This level of automation was the engine of speed. It allowed companies to release updates safely and reliably multiple times a day, responding to customer feedback or fixing a bug in a matter of hours, not months.

This speed also demanded a new way of thinking about the architecture of the software itself. The monolithic applications of the on-premise era, where every feature was part of a single, tightly coupled codebase, were too fragile for this new world. A small bug in one minor feature could bring the entire system crashing down. The solution was the shift to a microservices architecture. This approach broke the monolith apart into a collection of small, independent services, each responsible for a single piece of business functionality. One microservice might handle user authentication, another might manage the billing process, and a third might be responsible for the search feature. Each of these services could be developed, tested, and deployed independently by a small, dedicated team. This architectural decoupling was a crucial enabler of organizational scaling, allowing dozens or even hundreds of teams to work on the same complex product in parallel without constantly stepping on each other's toes.

With the service running 24/7, a new discipline emerged to ensure it stayed that way. Pioneered by Google, Site Reliability Engineering (SRE) was a new approach to the age-old problem of operations. The core idea of SRE was to treat operations as a software engineering problem. Instead of manually configuring servers, an SRE team would write code to automate the provisioning and management of the infrastructure. They lived by a strict "error budget," a concept that defined an acceptable level of unavailability for the service. As long as the service was meeting its reliability targets, the development teams were free to launch new features. If a series of bad deployments caused the system to exceed its error budget, all new feature launches were frozen until the underlying reliability issues were fixed. This created a powerful, data-driven balance between the competing needs of innovation and stability.

This data-driven mindset permeated every aspect of the modern SaaS organization, most notably in the role of the product manager. The product managers of the cloud era were a different breed from their on-premise predecessors. Their job was not simply to act as a scribe for customer feature requests. They were now expected to be the CEO of their feature, armed with a deep understanding of the customer, the business, and, most importantly, the data. Decisions were no longer made based on the opinion of the highest-paid person in the room. They were made based on evidence.

The new product management toolkit was one of experimentation. Before committing to building a major new feature, a team might first run an A/B test, showing a prototype of the feature to a small percentage of users to see if it actually moved the needle on a key metric like engagement or conversion. They would pore over product analytics dashboards to understand how users were actually behaving inside the application, identifying points of friction and opportunities for improvement. They would spend countless hours on calls with customers, not just asking them what they wanted, but digging deep to understand the underlying "job to be done." The goal was no longer to simply ship features on a roadmap; it was to achieve measurable business outcomes.

To achieve this level of speed and customer-centricity, the very structure of the organization had to be re-imagined. The rigid, hierarchical silos of the past were too slow and bureaucratic. The new model, which became the template for countless high-growth startups, was one of small, autonomous, cross-functional teams. Amazon famously codified this as the "two-pizza team" rule: if a team was too big to be fed by two pizzas, it was too big. The ideal team was a self-contained unit, typically consisting of a product manager, a designer, and a handful of engineers, all sitting together and completely dedicated to a single mission or a specific area of the product.

Perhaps the most influential articulation of this new organizational philosophy came from the music streaming giant Spotify. They developed a model that became the envy of the tech world, organizing their teams into "Squads, Tribes, Chapters, and Guilds." A Squad was the basic unit, a small, two-pizza team that was autonomous and self-organizing. A collection of squads working in a related area formed a Tribe. To ensure that engineers with the same skills could share knowledge and best practices across different squads, they were also part of a Chapter (e.g., the front-end engineering chapter or the data science chapter). Finally, Guilds were lightweight communities of interest, open to anyone who wanted to share knowledge on a topic like web performance or a new programming language. This matrix-like structure was a brilliant attempt to achieve the holy grail of organizational design: a company that could scale to thousands of employees while retaining the agility and innovative spirit of a small startup.

A key tenet of this new culture was the belief that customer empathy was everyone's job. It could not be delegated solely to the Customer Success department. The best SaaS companies found creative ways to immerse their entire organization in the customer's world. A common practice was "all hands support," a rotation that required everyone in the company, from the newest marketing hire to the CEO, to spend a few hours each quarter answering customer support tickets. This practice had a powerful effect. An engineer who had just spent an hour struggling to explain a confusing part of the user interface to a frustrated customer was far more motivated to go back and fix it than one who had only read about the problem in a bug report. It created a visceral, human connection to the impact of their work and closed the gap between the builders and the users.

This intense, fast-paced, and mission-driven environment created a fierce war for talent. The venture capital flooding the industry meant that a talented engineer or product manager had their choice of dozens of well-funded, ambitious startups. In this hyper-competitive market, compensation became more than just a salary. The key weapon in the recruiting arsenal was equity. Stock options were not just a financial instrument; they were a core part of the cultural promise. The pitch to a potential employee was not just to come and do a job, but to become an owner, to be part of a small team with the chance to build something massive and share in the wealth created. This ownership mentality was a powerful motivator, aligning the interests of the employees with the long-term success of the company.

The greatest challenge for these rapidly growing empires was figuring out how to maintain this special cultural DNA as they scaled. The scrappy, informal, all-hands-on-deck culture of a fifty-person startup is a fragile thing. It can easily be crushed under the weight of the processes, hierarchies, and communication overhead that inevitably come with growth. The companies that navigated this transition successfully did so with deliberate intent. They didn't just let their culture happen; they actively designed it.

This involved codifying the core values that defined them, not as platitudes on a poster, but as a practical guide for making decisions and hiring new people. A company like Netflix became famous for its detailed culture deck, which explicitly laid out its philosophy on concepts like "freedom and responsibility" and "context, not control." Leaders focused on radical transparency, sharing company financials, board meeting decks, and strategic plans with the entire company to ensure everyone felt like a trusted insider. They invested heavily in their hiring processes, optimizing for candidates who not only had the right skills but who also resonated with the company's core values. They understood that in the long run, culture was not just a part of the strategy; it was the strategy. The cloud empires were built on code and funded by capital, but they were animated and sustained by the unique cultures of the teams that brought them to life.

CHAPTER NINETEEN: Global Domination: The International Expansion of SaaS

For the first generation of cloud entrepreneurs, the world felt exhilaratingly and deceptively flat. The internet was a great equalizer, a global distribution channel that required no shipping containers, no customs declarations, and no overseas factories. A developer in Palo Alto could write a piece of code, deploy it to a server in Virginia, and, in theory, sell it to a customer in Stockholm as easily as one in St. Louis. This frictionless ideal was a core part of the SaaS promise. Many startups experienced this firsthand, often by accident. They would launch their service, focused entirely on their domestic market, only to find a curious collection of international flags appearing in their customer analytics. A small design firm in the Netherlands, a freelance accountant in Australia, a marketing team in Brazil—all had found their way to the website via a Google search, signed up with a credit card, and become paying customers without ever speaking to a human being.

This "accidental" international presence was a tantalizing glimpse of the potential scale of the cloud. It proved that the problems these new applications were solving were not unique to one country; they were universal pains felt by businesses everywhere. However, this passive, inbound trickle of global customers was a far cry from a true international strategy. It was a sign of opportunity, but not a plan to capture it. To transform from a domestic success story into a genuine cloud empire required a conscious, deliberate, and often perilous leap across borders. The decision to go global was not a matter of if, but when and how. The "when" was often triggered by a dawning realization that even the vast North American market was finite. As growth in their home territory began to slow, ambitious founders and their venture capital backers would look at a world map and see that the majority of their Total Addressable Market lay outside their current reach. The "how" was infinitely more complex.

The first and most obvious hurdle was language. Translating a website and a user interface into a new language seemed like a straightforward first step. Yet this task, known in the industry as localization, quickly revealed itself to be a treacherous minefield of nuance. A direct, literal translation often resulted in a product that felt awkward, unprofessional, or, in the worst cases, nonsensical. Idiomatic expressions, cultural references, and even the tone of voice had to be carefully adapted, or "transcreated," by native speakers who understood the local business culture. This was not a one-time project. Every new feature, every marketing email, and every support article had to be run through this same complex localization pipeline, adding a significant layer of operational overhead.

Beyond the words on the screen, the product itself had to be adapted to the simple, yet maddeningly diverse, realities of global commerce. A user in the United States expects to see dates written as month/day/year and prices in dollars, denoted with a ".". A user in Germany expects day.month.year and prices in Euros, denoted with a "," as the decimal separator. An accounting software platform that couldn't handle Value Added Tax (VAT) was useless in Europe. A CRM that couldn't properly process names written in Japanese Kanji characters was a non-starter in Japan. These seemingly small details were absolute deal-breakers. The product had to be re-engineered from the ground up to support internationalization, a process that involved everything from changing how data was stored in the database to allowing for different currencies and tax systems.

The go-to-market playbook, so carefully honed in the domestic market, often proved to be a poor fit for new territories. The inbound content marketing machine that worked so brilliantly in the English-speaking world had to be completely rebuilt. It wasn't enough to translate existing blog posts; a new content strategy had to be created, one that addressed the specific pain points and search terms of customers in each new market. The digital channels themselves were different. While Google was a dominant force in many countries, a company expanding into Russia had to contend with Yandex, and in China, Baidu was king. The social media landscape was equally fragmented, with platforms like WeChat, LINE, and VKontakte holding sway in their respective regions.

The sales process also required a radical rethink. The high-velocity, metric-driven inside sales model, perfected in the hyper-competitive American market, did not always translate well to cultures where business was built on long-term relationships and face-to-face trust. In many parts of Asia and Europe, a deal was less likely to be closed over a Zoom call and more likely to be sealed over a long lunch. This often necessitated a move away from the purely inside sales model and a significant investment in building a local "field" sales team, a costly proposition that dramatically altered the unit economics of the business. Even the concept of a free trial or a freemium product, the engine of product-led growth, could be met with skepticism in markets that were not accustomed to the "try before you buy" ethos of Silicon Valley.

Navigating the financial and legal landscape of each new country was another labyrinth. Setting up a local business entity, opening a bank account, and complying with local labor laws was a complex and time-consuming process that required expensive local expertise. Accepting payments became a major challenge. While Stripe had made credit card processing simple in many parts of the world, it was not ubiquitous. In the Netherlands, iDEAL was the dominant form of online payment. In Germany, many customers preferred direct bank transfers. A SaaS company that could not offer the preferred local payment method was creating a massive point of friction right at the most critical moment of the sale.

Looming over all of this was the ever-growing patchwork of data privacy and sovereignty regulations. As we saw in a previous chapter, laws like GDPR forced a fundamental change in how companies handled customer data. For an expanding SaaS business, this meant making critical, and expensive, strategic decisions. To sell to European customers, it was no longer enough to just have a German-language website; many large enterprise customers now demanded that their data be physically stored in a data center on European soil. This forced SaaS companies to abandon the simplicity of a single, centralized infrastructure and move to a multi-region architecture, deploying copies of their application in AWS or Azure data centers in Frankfurt, Dublin, or Paris. This added immense technical complexity and cost, but it became the non-negotiable price of entry into the lucrative European market.

Faced with this daunting array of challenges, SaaS companies developed several distinct playbooks for their global expansion. One of the most common was the "beachhead" strategy. Instead of attempting a simultaneous global assault, a company would pick a single, strategic market to enter first. For American companies, this was often the United Kingdom. The shared language and similar business culture made it a relatively low-friction first step, allowing the company to learn the basics of international operations—hiring overseas, dealing with new currencies, navigating different regulations—before tackling the greater complexities of non-English-speaking markets.

A company that exemplified this methodical approach was HubSpot. After establishing dominance in the North American market for inbound marketing software, they made a deliberate push into Europe. They chose Dublin, Ireland, as their EMEA headquarters, drawn by its favorable corporate tax rates and its deep pool of multilingual talent. From this base, they began a systematic process of localization. They didn't just translate their software; they translated their entire educational ecosystem. They created "HubSpot Academy" courses in German, French, and Spanish. They launched local-language blogs with content tailored to the specific challenges of marketers in each country. This deep investment in providing value before extracting it allowed them to replicate their successful inbound model across the continent.

Another popular strategy was to rely on a network of channel partners. Instead of building their own sales and support teams from scratch in a new country, a SaaS company could partner with an established local firm—a reseller, a consultant, or a system integrator—that already had a deep understanding of the market and a roster of existing customers. This could dramatically accelerate market entry and reduce the initial financial risk. The downside, of course, was a loss of control. The SaaS company was now one step removed from its end customers, and it had to share a significant portion of its revenue with the partner. For many, however, this was a worthwhile trade-off for speed and local expertise. Salesforce, in its global expansion, masterfully blended a direct sales force with a vast ecosystem of local implementation partners who were essential for its success in complex enterprise deals.

For the new generation of product-led growth companies, the product itself became the primary vehicle for international expansion. A tool like Slack or Trello, available for free, could cross borders effortlessly. It would be adopted by a small team in Tokyo, a startup in São Paulo, or a university department in Milan, all without any direct sales or marketing effort from the company. This organic, bottom-up adoption created a real-time map of global demand. The company could simply look at its usage data to see which countries had the highest concentration of engaged free users. These "PQLs" (Product Qualified Leads) in a new country were a powerful signal that the market was ripe for a more focused investment, justifying the cost of hiring a local team and launching a targeted marketing campaign. Atlassian, the Australian software giant, built a multi-billion dollar empire on this model, acquiring customers in virtually every country on earth with a famously small traditional sales team.

The boldest, and often riskiest, path to global expansion was through acquisition. A well-funded company could shortcut the entire painful learning process by simply buying a local competitor that had already figured out the product, the go-to-market strategy, and the cultural nuances of a target region. This provided instant market share and an experienced local team. However, it was also a strategy fraught with peril. The financial cost was often immense, and the challenge of integrating the technology and, more importantly, the culture of two different companies from opposite sides of the world could be a recipe for disaster.

As the SaaS industry matured, these playbooks became more sophisticated. A successful global strategy was rarely a matter of choosing one path, but of blending several. A company might use a PLG model to seed a new market, then hire a small local team to convert the largest of those organic users into enterprise accounts, while simultaneously building a network of channel partners to reach the broader mid-market. The process of going global became a core competency, a well-oiled machine that could be replicated for each new market entry. Companies created dedicated "internationalization" teams, composed of engineers, product managers, and marketers, whose sole job was to pave the way for the company's expansion.

This global push fundamentally reshaped the SaaS landscape. It turned the leading cloud companies into truly multinational corporations, with offices and employees scattered across every time zone. It forced a new level of sophistication in product architecture and organizational design. And it created a virtuous cycle of its own. As SaaS platforms became global standards, they, in turn, enabled a new generation of startups to be "born global" from day one. An entrepreneur building on top of AWS, Stripe, and Shopify could now launch an e-commerce business that could sell to and accept payments from customers anywhere in the world, leveraging the global infrastructure that the first wave of cloud empires had spent a decade and billions of dollars to build. The world was not as flat as the early pioneers had dreamed, but the SaaS revolution had provided the tools to navigate its complex and varied terrain.

CHAPTER TWENTY: The Dark Side of the Cloud: Vendor Lock-In and Data Privacy Concerns

For every celebrated advantage of the cloud, for every tale of frictionless scaling and newfound agility, there exists a shadow narrative, a quiet accounting of the compromises made and the control relinquished. The revolution that liberated businesses from the tyranny of their own server rooms did not eliminate power dynamics; it simply relocated them. The promise of renting software like a utility was brilliantly simple, but it obscured a more complex reality. When you rent, the landlord sets the rules. The cloud empires were built on a grand bargain: in exchange for unprecedented convenience and power, customers would agree to live within the walls of a new kind of digital estate, one whose gates were often much harder to leave than they first appeared.

This subtle but powerful form of captivity is known as vendor lock-in. It is not a conspiracy, but rather the natural and intended outcome of a well-designed business strategy. The goal of any cloud platform is to make itself indispensable, to weave its services so deeply into the operational fabric of a customer's business that the prospect of leaving becomes technically, financially, and organizationally unthinkable. This is not achieved through ironclad, multi-decade contracts, but through a far more effective mechanism: the deliberate creation of immense switching costs. The cage is not built of iron bars, but of intricate, golden threads of convenience.

The first layer of lock-in is forged in the very foundations of the cloud, at the Infrastructure as a Service (IaaS) layer. The three giants—AWS, Azure, and Google Cloud—all offer a set of core, commodity services like virtual servers (EC2, Azure VMs, Compute Engine) and basic storage (S3, Blob Storage, Cloud Storage). In theory, an application built using only these generic building blocks could be moved from one cloud to another with a manageable amount of effort. This theoretical portability, however, is a siren song that few modern applications heed. The real power, and the real stickiness, of these platforms lies in their vast and ever-growing catalogs of higher-level, proprietary services.

A development team, under pressure to build and ship features quickly, will rarely choose the harder, more portable path. Why build and manage your own database cluster on a generic virtual server when you can use Amazon's Aurora or Google's Spanner, which offer superior performance and are managed for you? Why construct a complex data analytics pipeline from scratch when you can simply pipe everything into Google BigQuery or Amazon Redshift? Each of these decisions, perfectly rational and efficient in the moment, is another thread in the web of lock-in. The application becomes a complex tapestry woven from dozens of these proprietary APIs. To migrate to a competing cloud would not be a simple "lift and shift"; it would require a fundamental and costly re-architecture of the entire system.

This dynamic is even more pronounced at the Software as a Service (SaaS) layer. Here, the lock-in is not just about code and APIs; it is about the most valuable and inert asset a company possesses: its data. This phenomenon is known as "data gravity." Over years of operation, a company will pour an immense volume of information into its core systems of record. Its entire sales history, every customer interaction, and every support ticket lives inside Salesforce. Its complete financial ledger, every invoice and every expense report, resides in NetSuite. Its human resources data, every employee record and every payroll run, is managed by Workday.

While these platforms provide APIs to export this data, an export is not the same as an escape. The raw data, stripped of the context, the relationships, and the intricate customizations of the platform it was born in, is often of limited use. Migrating this data to a new, competing system is a Herculean task, fraught with the risk of data loss and corruption. The process often requires months of planning, specialized consultants, and a painstaking mapping of data fields from the old system to the new. For a business in motion, the prospect of undertaking such a high-risk, resource-intensive "heart transplant" is terrifying enough to keep them paying their subscription fees, even in the face of rising prices or declining satisfaction.

The API economy, the celebrated engine of interconnection, ironically becomes a powerful agent of lock-in. As a company adopts more best-of-breed SaaS tools, it builds a complex web of integrations that all orbit around a central "sun," which is typically its primary CRM or ERP system. The marketing automation platform syncs with the CRM, which in turn syncs with the helpdesk software, which then connects to the accounting system. This interconnected digital nervous system is highly efficient, but also brittle. Ripping out the central platform is no longer about replacing one system; it is about rebuilding dozens of critical workflows that the business relies on to function. The switching cost is not just the cost of the new software; it is the cost of re-plumbing the entire organization.

This inability to easily leave has predictable economic consequences. Once a vendor knows a customer is locked in, the power dynamic of the relationship shifts. The friendly, flexible sales process that characterized the initial courtship is often replaced by a far more rigid and demanding negotiation upon renewal. Price increases that far exceed the rate of inflation become common. The leverage has shifted to the landlord, who knows that the cost of moving out is far greater than the cost of a rent hike. This can also lead to a decline in innovation and responsiveness. A company that does not have to constantly fight to re-earn its customers' business has less incentive to invest in improving its product or providing world-class support.

The second, and perhaps more troubling, dark side of the cloud lies in the realm of privacy. The very architecture that makes SaaS so efficient—the centralized, multi-tenant database—also creates a profound and unsettling concentration of risk. In the on-premise world, a data breach at one company affected only that company. In the cloud, a single successful attack on a major SaaS provider can expose the sensitive data of thousands of businesses in one catastrophic event. This centralization of data creates an irresistible target for hackers, a digital Fort Knox that is under constant siege. While the leading cloud providers invest billions in security, the sheer value of the prize ensures that the attackers will be equally well-funded and relentless.

Beyond the risk of external attack, a more fundamental question has emerged about the nature of data ownership in the cloud. When a company uploads its data to a SaaS platform, it is entering into a complex and often opaque relationship. The terms of service, which few people ever read, frequently grant the provider broad rights to use, analyze, and derive insights from this data, as long as it is anonymized and aggregated. This "data exhaust" is the raw material that fuels the vendor's own research and development. The customer's operational data is used to train the machine learning models that power the platform's next generation of "intelligent" features, which are then sold back to the customer as a premium add-on.

In this model, the customer is not just a user of the software; they are an unwitting and unpaid supplier of the very resource that creates the vendor's most powerful competitive advantage. The data network effect, celebrated as a brilliant business moat, is built on this foundation. The more customers a platform has, the more data it collects, the smarter its AI gets, and the more difficult it becomes for a new competitor to challenge it. The customers themselves are actively, if unknowingly, reinforcing the walls of the very platform that may be locking them in.

This vast concentration of data in the hands of a few, predominantly American, tech giants has also attracted the intense and unwelcome attention of governments around the world. As discussed previously, laws like the US CLOUD Act create a direct conflict between the legal obligations of a US-based tech company and the privacy rights of its international customers. A warrant from a US court can compel a provider like Microsoft or Amazon to hand over the data of a European corporation, even if that data is stored on a server in Frankfurt. This capability has led to a deep and abiding mistrust among international regulators and has fueled the push toward data localization and a "splinternet" divided along geopolitical lines.

The privacy implications extend beyond the direct customer to the customers of the customer. A typical CRM system contains the personally identifiable information (PII) of every individual a company has ever interacted with. This creates a vast, interconnected shadow profile of millions of people, managed by a third-party vendor with its own security vulnerabilities and business imperatives. An individual has no direct relationship with the SaaS provider that holds their data, and often has no idea it is even there. Their ability to control their own information is entirely dependent on the diligence and the policies of a company they have never heard of.

As Artificial Intelligence becomes more deeply woven into the fabric of SaaS applications, a new set of privacy and ethical challenges is emerging. An AI-powered HR platform that analyzes employee behavior to predict who is a "flight risk" may create a more efficient business, but it does so by subjecting employees to a new and invisible form of algorithmic surveillance. An AI that scores sales leads based on thousands of data points may be highly effective, but it can also perpetuate and amplify existing societal biases, all within the impenetrable confines of a "black box" algorithm. When the software starts making autonomous judgments about people, questions of fairness, transparency, and accountability become paramount.

This is the great, unspoken trade-off of the cloud. The journey to the cloud is a one-way street for most. The convenience, the scalability, and the raw power are undeniable and, for most businesses, irresistible. But the price of this power is a subtle but significant transfer of control. It is a pact in which businesses gain the ability to move faster and see farther, but in doing so, they become tenants in an empire they did not build and whose rules they cannot write. The cloud is not a malevolent force, but it is not a neutral one either. It is an architecture of power, and like any concentration of power, its benefits are immense, its allure is undeniable, and its consequences are profound and far-reaching.

CHAPTER TWENTY-ONE: The Serverless Future: The Evolution of Cloud Infrastructure

The great promise of the cloud was the elimination of the server. Not the physical machine itself, of course—somewhere, in a vast and windowless building, a fan was still spinning—but the elimination of the *idea* of the server as a problem for the developer. The Infrastructure as a Service revolution was the first, giant leap in this direction. It transformed the weeks-long ordeal of procuring a physical server into a five-minute API call. It was a miracle of abstraction. Yet, for all its power, it did not fully vanquish the ghost in the machine. It simply replaced a physical server with a virtual one.

This virtual server, this EC2 instance or Azure VM, was a vast improvement, but it was still, fundamentally, a server. It had an operating system that needed to be patched. It had capacity that needed to be managed. It had to be monitored, secured, and, most maddeningly, paid for, whether it was busy or not. A company that launched a new photo-sharing app might provision a cluster of virtual servers to handle the expected load. But at three in the morning, when most of its users were asleep, those servers would sit largely idle, humming away in a data center, their virtual meters ticking away, consuming cash. The tyranny of the idle server was the cloud's last great inefficiency, a faint but persistent echo of the old on-premise world.

The problem was one of mismatched scale. An application doesn't run continuously; it runs in response to events. A user clicks a button, an image is uploaded, a purchase is made. The software only needs to work for the brief, fleeting moments that these events occur. The infrastructure, however, was stubbornly continuous, a block of rented compute power leased by the hour. The next great evolutionary leap in cloud infrastructure would come from a movement that sought to perfectly align the two, to atomize the very concept of computing down to its most essential component. The goal was to stop renting the kitchen and to start paying only for the meal. This was the dawn of serverless.

The name, of course, is a brilliant and slightly misleading piece of marketing. Serverless computing is not a world without servers. It is a world where a developer can, for the first time, write and deploy code without ever having to think about a server again. It is the final and most complete layer of abstraction. The cloud provider assumes the entire burden of managing the underlying infrastructure: the provisioning, the scaling, the patching, the entire operational headache. The developer is left with only one responsibility: writing the code that delivers business value. The unit of deployment is no longer a machine or a container; it is simply a function.

This new paradigm was formally christened "Functions as a Service," or FaaS, and its arrival was heralded by the launch of a quietly revolutionary service from Amazon Web Services in 2014: AWS Lambda. The concept was simple and profound. A developer could write a small, self-contained piece of code—a function—that was designed to perform a single task. This function would then lie dormant, costing nothing, until it was awakened by a specific, pre defined trigger. That trigger could be almost anything: an HTTP request from a user clicking a link, a new photo being uploaded to an S3 storage bucket, a new record being added to a database, or a simple timer firing every hour.

When the trigger event occurred, the magic happened. In the background, AWS would instantly find an available slice of compute power, execute the function's code, and then shut it down. The entire process might last only a few hundred milliseconds. The billing model was the true revolution. The customer was charged only for the precise number of milliseconds their code was actually running, and a nominal fee for each time it was invoked. The cost of idle was not just minimized; it was eliminated entirely. For the first time, compute was a true utility, billed with the same granular precision as electricity from a power grid. You only paid for the light when the switch was on.

This event-driven model unlocked a new and far more efficient way of building applications. The classic example that became the "Hello, World!" of the serverless era was image processing. In the old model, if you wanted to create thumbnails for every photo a user uploaded, you would need a server (or a fleet of them) constantly running, polling a storage directory to see if a new image had arrived. It was a clumsy and wasteful process. With serverless, the workflow became elegant and effortless. The developer would write a simple Lambda function that takes an image, resizes it, and saves the thumbnails. They would then configure that function to be triggered by a "new object" event in their S3 bucket. From that moment on, every time a user uploaded a photo, the function would automatically and instantly spring to life, create the thumbnails, and go back to sleep. The system could handle one upload a day or a million uploads an hour, and the developer had to do nothing to scale it. The cloud provider handled it all.

This automatic, instantaneous scaling was the superpower of the serverless model. For applications with unpredictable or "spiky" traffic patterns, it was a game-changer. Imagine a startup running a live-voting application for a television show. For most of the week, the application would have zero traffic. But for a five-minute window during the show's broadcast, it would be hit with millions of concurrent requests. In the IaaS world, preparing for this would be a nightmare of overprovisioning, requiring a massive fleet of servers to be spun up and paid for, just to handle that brief, intense spike. With a serverless architecture, each vote could be handled by a separate function invocation. The system would scale from zero to millions of concurrent executions in seconds, and then scale back down to zero just as quickly, with the company paying only for the compute power used during those five frantic minutes.

To understand how this was possible required a peek behind the curtain. The cloud providers were not magically creating servers out of thin air. They were using a sophisticated form of containerization, maintaining a massive "warm pool" of generic compute environments, ready to be assigned a piece of code at a moment's notice. When an event was triggered, the provider would grab one of these warm containers, load the function's code into it, execute it, and then, after a short period, return the container to the pool.

This process, however, exposed the primary trade-off of the serverless model: the "cold start." If a function had not been invoked recently, there might not be a warm container immediately available for it. In this case, the provider would have to create a new one from scratch, a process that could introduce a noticeable delay, or latency, of a few hundred milliseconds or more. For many applications, this was completely imperceptible. But for a user-facing system that required an instantaneous response, like a high-frequency trading platform, this occasional latency could be a deal-breaker. Managing and mitigating cold starts became a new and important discipline for serverless engineers.

As the movement gained momentum, the term "serverless" expanded beyond just Functions as a Service. It evolved into a broader architectural philosophy centered on composing applications out of managed services. FaaS was the custom logic, the "glue," but the rest of the application could be built by stitching together other services that did not require server management. The ecosystem of these building blocks exploded.

Serverless databases like Amazon DynamoDB and Google Firestore offered a place to store data that scaled automatically, with billing based on read and write operations, not on the uptime of a database server. Services like Amazon API Gateway allowed developers to create and manage robust APIs where each endpoint could be wired directly to a Lambda function. Authentication became a managed service with tools like Auth0 and AWS Cognito, which handled the entire complex process of user sign-ups, logins, and security. Even the original cloud service, AWS S3, came to be seen as the quintessential serverless offering—a place to store a virtually infinite number of files without ever thinking about a single disk drive.

Using this palette of managed services, a developer could now construct a highly sophisticated, globally scalable, and remarkably cost-effective application without ever once having to SSH into a Linux machine or apply a security patch. The developer's role was elevated. They were no longer a system administrator; they were an architect, a cloud plumber connecting a series of powerful, pre-built components and writing only the unique business logic that made their application special.

This new way of building, however, came with its own set of formidable challenges. The first was a dramatic increase in complexity. A traditional monolithic application, for all its faults, was easy to reason about and debug. It was one big thing. A serverless application, by contrast, was a highly distributed system, a constellation of dozens or even hundreds of tiny, interconnected functions and services. Tracing a single user request as it bounced from an API Gateway endpoint to a Lambda function, which then wrote to a DynamoDB table, which in turn triggered another function, became a serious challenge. This gave rise to a new generation of "observability" platforms, SaaS tools specifically designed to provide visibility into these complex, event-driven architectures.

The second and more strategic challenge was a supercharged version of an old problem: vendor lock-in. If an application built on proprietary IaaS services was difficult to move, a serverless application was welded to the platform it was built on. The function code itself might be portable, but the entire architecture was defined by the intricate web of triggers, permissions, and specific integrations between the provider's managed services. An application built on AWS Lambda, API Gateway, DynamoDB, and Cognito was not a generic "cloud" application; it was an AWS application. Moving it to Google Cloud or Microsoft Azure would be less of a migration and more of a complete rewrite from the ground up. This was the grand bargain of serverless: in exchange for the ultimate level of abstraction and operational freedom, you agreed to build your house deeper inside the vendor's walled garden than ever before.

Despite these challenges, the serverless model represented a clear and compelling direction for the future of the cloud. It was the logical conclusion of the journey that began with the first virtual machine. It shifted the economic model of software from one of ownership, to rental, and finally to pure consumption. It forced developers to think in a new way, to break down complex problems into small, discrete, event-driven units. It created a new kind of developer, one who spent less time worrying about the plumbing of the internet and more time focused on the one thing that truly mattered: writing the code that solves a customer's problem.

CHAPTER TWENTY-TWO: The Edge Computing Frontier: Decentralizing the Cloud

For twenty-one chapters, we have charted the relentless march toward centralization. The story of the cloud has been a story of consolidation, a great digital migration from millions of scattered, private server closets into a few dozen colossal, hyper-scale data centers. These digital cathedrals, operated by a tiny handful of tech titans, became the new centers of the computational universe. The model was built on the brute-force logic of economies of scale: it was cheaper, more efficient, and more powerful to bring the world's data to a central brain for processing. For a vast class of applications, this model was, and remains, a triumph. But the universe, it turns out, has a speed limit, and the physical laws of latency and bandwidth were about to stage a quiet rebellion.

The centralized cloud, for all its power, operates under a fundamental physical constraint: the speed of light. Data cannot travel faster than photons through a fiber optic cable. For a user in Singapore to access a service running on a server in Virginia, the data must embark on a round-trip journey of thousands of miles. Even at light speed, this trip takes time—a few hundred milliseconds of delay, known as latency. For sending an email, updating a CRM record, or streaming a movie, this brief delay is completely imperceptible. But a new generation of technology was emerging for which a delay of even a few dozen milliseconds was the difference between a magical experience and a useless one. The central brain was too slow; the world needed reflexes.

This realization gave birth to a new and seemingly paradoxical movement: the decentralization of the cloud. This was the dawn of edge computing. The core idea is not to replace the centralized cloud, but to augment and extend it. Edge computing is a philosophy of location. It seeks to move compute power and data storage away from the distant, centralized data centers and closer to the physical location where data is being generated and consumed. It is an acknowledgment that not all data is created equal. Some of it needs to be processed immediately, right where the action is. The cloud was no longer to be a single, distant destination; it was to become a distributed continuum, stretching from the core data center all the way to the very edge of the network.

The most immediate and obvious driver for this shift was the latency problem. Consider the dream of the truly autonomous vehicle. A self-driving car navigating a chaotic city street must make thousands of micro-decisions every second. It must identify a pedestrian stepping off a curb, predict their path, and apply the brakes in a fraction of a second. The car cannot afford to send a video feed to a data center five hundred miles away, wait for an AI model to analyze it, and receive an instruction to brake. The decision must be made instantly, "on the edge," by powerful computers located inside the vehicle itself. The laws of physics demand local processing.

This same need for instantaneous response is the engine behind the immersive worlds of augmented and virtual reality. For an AR headset to convincingly overlay digital information onto your view of the real world, it must track your head movements with microscopic precision and render the graphics with near-zero delay. Any perceptible lag between your movement and the visual update results in a jarring, disorienting experience that can quickly lead to motion sickness. To create a seamless illusion, the immense computational work of rendering these digital worlds must happen either on the device itself or on a server located extremely close by, perhaps in the same building or at the nearest 5G cell tower.

The second great force pushing computation to the edge was the sheer, overwhelming deluge of data. The centralized cloud model was built on the assumption that it was practical to move data to the compute. The Internet of Things (IoT) shattered that assumption. A modern factory floor can be equipped with tens of thousands of sensors, monitoring the temperature, vibration, and performance of every machine. A single jet engine can generate terabytes of data on a single flight. A smart city might deploy thousands of high-definition cameras to monitor traffic flow. To stream all of this raw, unfiltered data back to a central cloud in real-time would be both astronomically expensive and technically impossible; there simply isn't enough bandwidth in the world.

Edge computing flips the model. Instead of moving the data to the compute, it moves the compute to the data. A small, powerful "edge gateway" server can be installed on the factory floor. This gateway ingests the constant firehose of sensor data, processes it locally, and runs machine learning models to look for anomalies that might predict a machine failure. For 99.9% of the time, the data is routine and can be discarded or summarized. Only the important events—the anomalies, the alerts, the critical insights— are sent back to the central cloud for long-term storage and deeper analysis. The edge acts as a smart, distributed filter for the physical world, reducing a torrent of raw data to a manageable stream of valuable information.

A third driver, intertwined with the regulatory landscape we have already explored, was the growing demand for data privacy and sovereignty. For certain sensitive applications, the data can never be allowed to leave the premises. A hospital, for example, might use AI-powered cameras to monitor patients in its intensive care unit. The video feeds from these cameras are protected health information and, due to both regulations like HIPAA and patient privacy concerns, cannot be streamed to a public cloud for analysis. An on-premise edge server can run the AI models locally, alerting nurses to a potential emergency without the sensitive video data ever leaving the hospital's secure network. The edge provides a way to get the benefits of cloud-native technology while respecting the strictest of data residency boundaries.

The "edge" is not a single location, but a spectrum. It is best understood as a multi-tiered hierarchy of compute, a series of concentric circles moving outward from the core. The innermost circle is the traditional, hyper-scale cloud data center. Moving outward, the next layer is the network or "near" edge. This consists of smaller data centers or points of presence located within a city, often inside the facilities of an internet service provider or a telecom company. Further out is the on-premise or "far" edge, which is the compute infrastructure located at the site where the data is generated—the factory, the retail store, the farm, the car. The final, outermost layer is the device edge, which is the computational power embedded within the IoT device or sensor itself.

This tiered architecture allows for a sophisticated distribution of workloads. A smart camera on a street corner (the device edge) might perform basic object detection, identifying that a car has passed. It sends this simple piece of metadata to a server at the base of the local cell tower (the network edge), which aggregates the data from hundreds of other cameras to calculate real-time traffic flow. At the end of the day, it sends a summary of the day's traffic patterns to the central cloud (the core) for historical analysis and urban planning. Each layer of the edge performs the work best suited to its location and capabilities.

This new frontier created a massive strategic battleground, attracting a diverse set of players, each hoping to stake a claim. The established IaaS giants were not about to let the world decentralize without them. Their strategy was to extend their existing cloud empires outward. They developed products like AWS Outposts, Microsoft Azure Stack, and Google Anthos, which are, in essence, racks of their own cloud hardware and software that a customer can install in their own data center or a co-location facility. This creates a "hybrid cloud," allowing a business to run workloads on the edge using the exact same APIs, tools, and management console they use for the public cloud. It's a powerful pitch: a single, consistent platform that stretches from their global data centers right into your server room.

The pioneers of the original edge, the Content Delivery Networks (CDNs), saw this new movement as a natural evolution of their business. Companies like Akamai and Cloudflare had already spent two decades building out a massive, global network of servers designed to cache static content like images and videos closer to end-users to make websites load faster. They realized that these thousands of distributed servers were the perfect real estate for running code. They began transforming their caching networks into global, serverless compute platforms. Services like Cloudflare Workers and Akamai's EdgeWorkers allow developers to deploy small, event-driven functions that execute on their edge servers, just milliseconds away from the end-user. For a global e-commerce site, this means they can run code to personalize the user experience or check inventory without ever having to make a slow, round-trip call back to a central server.

The telecommunications companies also saw a once-in-a-generation opportunity. The rollout of the 5G wireless network promised a world of ultra-low latency, but this promise could only be fulfilled if the compute was moved physically closer to the radio. This led to the rise of Multi-access Edge Computing, or MEC. The telcos, who own the real estate at the base of the cell towers, began partnering with the cloud giants to install small-scale cloud data centers directly inside their network infrastructure. This allows a mobile application developer to deploy their code at the very edge of the 5G network, enabling a new class of applications, from real-time multiplayer mobile gaming to connected drones, that require an almost instantaneous response.

Finally, the hardware manufacturers that create the silicon brains of these systems found themselves at the center of a new gold rush. The edge is a world of constraints; devices often have limited power, are exposed to the elements, and need to perform complex tasks with high efficiency. This created a huge demand for specialized chips. NVIDIA, the leader in GPUs for the data center, developed a new line of smaller, power-efficient processors designed to run sophisticated AI models on edge devices, from tiny drones to the complex computer vision systems in a modern supermarket. The very architecture of the cloud, once a story about software abstracting away the hardware, was suddenly once again a story about the unique capabilities of the silicon itself.

The serverless paradigm, which we explored in the previous chapter, proved to be the perfect programming model for this new, distributed world. The small, stateless, and event-driven nature of a FaaS function is an ideal fit for the resource-constrained and ephemeral nature of edge computing. The idea of deploying a complete virtual machine to a sensor on a windmill is nonsensical. But deploying a small, lightweight function that wakes up when the wind speed changes, logs the data, and goes back to sleep, is a perfect match. The combination of serverless functions and a globally distributed edge network represents a new and powerful architectural pattern for building the next generation of applications.

Of course, this decentralized frontier is not without its perils. The operational complexity of managing a fleet of thousands or even millions of distributed edge devices is an immense challenge. How do you securely deploy new software updates to all of them? How do you monitor their health and performance? How do you protect them from physical tampering? The attack surface of the network is no longer a few well-fortified data centers; it is a vast and porous collection of endpoints scattered across the physical world. A new suite of tools and platforms is emerging to tackle this problem of "edge orchestration," but it remains a significant hurdle.

The shift to the edge represents a profound rebalancing of the digital world. For two decades, the gravitational pull of the centralized cloud was irresistible. It re-shaped the entire software industry and the very nature of how we build and consume technology. Now, the laws of physics are beginning to pull back in the other direction. This is not a rejection of the cloud, but its maturation. The cloud is un-tethering itself from the data center, becoming a diffuse, intelligent fabric that is woven into the world around us. The empire is not shrinking; it is expanding, pushing its borders out to the farthest reaches of the network to meet the real world where it happens.

CHAPTER TWENTY-THREE: The Impact of AI on the Future of Software

The advent of the embedded AI assistant, the "copilot" now appearing in everything from word processors to complex CRM systems, represents the most visible edge of a tectonic shift. It is a friendly and useful introduction to a new era, the digital equivalent of a helpful passenger in the car, ready to navigate or adjust the radio. This metaphor, however, for all its utility, profoundly understates the scale of the coming transformation. The true impact of artificial intelligence on software will not be to provide a helpful assistant for the driver. It will be to rebuild the car from the ground up, to change its fuel source, and, ultimately, to fuse the driver and the vehicle into a single, collaborative entity. AI is not simply being added to software; it is becoming its fundamental substance.

For most of its history, business software has served as a digital filing cabinet. It has been a "system of record," a passive vessel for storing information about what has already happened. An ERP system records transactions, a CRM system records customer interactions, and an HR system records employee data. The SaaS revolution made these records universally accessible and collaborative, but their essential nature remained passive. The infusion of AI is now transforming these platforms from inert systems of record into proactive "systems of intelligence." The software is no longer just remembering the past; it is actively attempting to predict and shape the future.

This transition moves beyond the simple predictive analytics that characterized the first wave of AI in SaaS. It is not just about forecasting next quarter's sales or identifying a customer at risk of churn. The new generation of software will ingest a far broader spectrum of data, including unstructured information from news articles, social media, and even global weather patterns, to make complex, multi-faceted recommendations. Imagine a supply chain management platform that doesn't just track inventory levels. It monitors geopolitical news, detects a brewing labor strike at a key port, cross-references shipping manifests and weather forecasts, and then autonomously re-routes a dozen container ships to alternative ports, all while pre-booking new ground transportation and notifying the affected customers of a potential, but now mitigated, delay. The software is no longer a tool for managing the supply chain; it is an active participant in its orchestration.

Similarly, the future of marketing automation will move beyond simply nurturing leads with pre-programmed email sequences. It will become a system that is given a high-level goal, such as "increase conversion rates among mid-market C-level executives in the DACH region by 10%." The AI will then devise its own strategy. It will generate the ad copy and the visual assets, A/B test thousands of variations across different channels, analyze the sentiment of online conversations to adjust its messaging in real-time, and dynamically allocate its budget to the most effective campaigns, reporting back not on clicks and open rates, but on its progress toward the stated business outcome. The human marketer's role shifts from a hands-on campaign operator to a high-level strategist who sets the goals and constraints for their autonomous AI counterpart.

This evolution in capability necessitates a parallel evolution in how humans interact with the software itself. The graphical user interface, the landscape of windows, icons, menus, and pointers that has dominated computing for forty years, is beginning to dissolve. It was a brilliant solution for a world where humans had to manually command a dumb machine, clicking and dragging to specify every single action. As the machine becomes intelligent, this highly structured method of interaction becomes a cumbersome bottleneck. The future of the user experience is conversational and intentional.

We are already seeing the early stages of this with the rise of the Language User Interface (LUI). The "copilot" chat window is the Trojan horse for this new paradigm. Initially, it helps users find features or summarize information. Soon, it will become the primary, and for many tasks the only, way of interacting with the application. Instead of navigating a complex reporting module with a dozen filters and dropdown menus, a sales manager will simply type or speak, "Compare the performance of my top three account executives for the last two quarters on deals over $100k, and highlight any anomalies in their sales cycle length." The software will not just present a static dashboard; it will generate a dynamic, narrative report, complete with visualizations and plain-English insights, perhaps even suggesting specific coaching opportunities for each team member.

The next logical step beyond the LUI is the "autonomous interface," where the goal is to have no interface at all for routine tasks. The software becomes a true agent, acting on the user's behalf based on a set of pre-defined goals and an understanding of their intent. The interface becomes a place for setting objectives, managing exceptions, and reviewing outcomes, rather than a place for performing the work itself. An accounting system, for example, will no longer require a user to manually process invoices. It will automatically ingest invoices from an email inbox, validate them against purchase orders, check for anomalies, schedule the payment, and simply ask the human for a final approval on any transaction that falls outside of its confidence threshold. The human's role is elevated to one of oversight and judgment, intervening only when their uniquely human context is required.

This profound change in the user experience is mirrored by an equally profound change in the experience of the software creator. The very process of building software is being consumed and remade by artificial intelligence. For decades, developers have worked by manually translating human ideas into the rigid, unforgiving syntax of a programming language. AI-powered tools are now beginning to automate this translation process, creating a new, higher level of abstraction. The initial wave of this was AI-powered code completion, where tools like GitHub Copilot acted as an incredibly sophisticated autocomplete for developers. The next wave is far more ambitious.

The industry is moving rapidly toward a reality where AI agents can take a high-level product specification, written in natural language and accompanied by a few wireframes, and generate the vast majority of the application's code autonomously. A product manager could describe a new mobile application for event management, specifying its key features, user roles, and data requirements. An AI development agent would then generate the front-end code for iOS and Android, write the back-end APIs, design the database schema, and even create the initial automated test suite. The role of the human engineer in this process shifts from being a bricklayer to an architect. They are responsible for designing the overall system, making key architectural decisions, reviewing the AI's output for quality and security, and then focusing their own manual coding efforts on the most novel, complex, and business-critical parts of the system that lie beyond the AI's current capabilities.

Once deployed, this new generation of software will not be a static artifact that needs to be manually patched and updated. It will be a dynamic, self-managing system. AI-powered observability platforms will continuously monitor the application in production. When an unexpected error occurs, the AI will not just send an alert to a human engineer. It will analyze the logs, trace the error back to the specific lines of code that caused it, propose a fix, test that fix in a simulated environment, and, if it is confident in the solution, deploy the patch to production automatically. This concept of "self-healing" software will dramatically reduce downtime and free up engineering teams from the constant, reactive cycle of bug-fixing.

Beyond simply fixing itself, the software will also learn to optimize itself. By analyzing real-world usage patterns, an AI-powered system can identify performance bottlenecks and rewrite its own code to be more efficient. It could automatically reconfigure its database indexes to speed up common queries or adjust its resource allocation on the cloud to reduce its operating costs, all without human intervention. The application becomes a living system, constantly adapting to its environment to become more resilient and more efficient over time.

This fundamental shift in how software is built and operates will inevitably force a corresponding shift in how it is sold. The traditional per-user, per-month SaaS pricing model begins to break down in a world of autonomous software. If a single employee can command an AI agent to perform the work that previously required a team of ten, is the value based on the one user or the ten virtual agents? The logical evolution is a move toward pricing models that are based not on usage, but on outcomes.

A vendor of an AI-powered marketing platform might charge its customer a percentage of the marketing-generated revenue it produces. An AI supply chain optimizer could be priced based on a share of the documented cost savings it achieves. This creates the ultimate alignment between the vendor and the customer. The software vendor is no longer selling a tool; they are selling a guaranteed business result. This value-based pricing is the commercial holy grail, but it requires a level of trust, transparency, and data-sharing that will push the vendor-customer relationship into a much deeper form of partnership.

Another emerging business model is "Model-as-a-Service," or MaaS. In this scenario, the most valuable asset a company possesses is not its application's code, but its proprietary, fine-tuned AI model, which has been trained on a unique and massive dataset. The company can then sell access to this model's intelligence via an API. Other companies can then build their own applications on top of this intelligence. A company that has spent years developing a world-class AI model for medical diagnosis, for example, might sell API access to that model to hospital systems, insurance companies, and telehealth startups, each of whom will use that core intelligence to power their own unique services. The competitive moat is the model itself, a product of the data network effect that is incredibly difficult for a competitor to replicate.

However, this AI-driven future is not a technological utopia. It comes with a new and formidable set of ethical and practical challenges. The problem of algorithmic bias is paramount. An AI model trained on historical data will inevitably learn and, in many cases, amplify the biases present in that data. An AI-powered recruiting tool trained on the hiring decisions of a historically male-dominated industry may learn to favor male candidates, creating a powerful engine for digital discrimination. SaaS vendors will be forced to invest heavily in techniques for bias detection and mitigation, and "AI fairness" will become a critical and marketable feature.

The "black box" problem presents another major hurdle. Many of the most powerful AI models are so complex that even their creators do not fully understand the specific reasoning behind any given decision. When an AI denies a loan application or flags a transaction as fraudulent, the business using that software may be legally required to provide an explanation. The demand for "Explainable AI" (XAI), systems that can articulate the logic behind their recommendations in a human-understandable way, will grow from an academic curiosity into a commercial necessity, particularly in regulated fields like finance and healthcare.

Finally, there is the undeniable societal impact. The technologies that will power the next generation of cloud empires are poised to automate not just the repetitive tasks of the factory floor, but the complex cognitive tasks of the knowledge worker. The roles of financial analysts, paralegals, marketers, and even software developers will be profoundly reshaped. This will create immense productivity gains and unlock new forms of creativity, but it will also cause significant economic dislocation. The software industry, for so long a pure engine of job creation, is now creating tools that have the potential to automate many of the very jobs it once supported. The conversation about the future of software is now inextricably linked to the conversation about the future of work itself.

CHAPTER TWENTY-FOUR: Web3 and the Decentralized Application Wave

For more than two decades, the digital world has been shaped by a powerful, centralizing gravity. The cloud empires, built on the logic of immense scale, pulled the world's data and computation into a handful of fortified, hyper-efficient data centers. This concentration of power was the engine of the SaaS revolution, enabling a world of accessible, powerful, and always-on software. But as this new order solidified, a quiet but persistent critique began to grow, a digital counterculture born from the very network the giants had come to dominate. The critique was aimed at the fundamental architecture of this new world: its reliance on trusted, centralized intermediaries.

This Web2 paradigm, the read-write web of platforms, was a vast improvement on the static, read-only web that preceded it. But its convenience came at a price. The platforms that hosted our conversations, stored our photos, and managed our businesses became the de facto arbiters of the digital world. They owned the servers, they controlled the data, and they set the rules. This created a new set of dependencies. A user's digital identity was tied to their Google or Facebook login. A startup's entire existence depended on the continued benevolence of Amazon Web Services. A creator's livelihood could be upended by a sudden change in YouTube's algorithm or Apple's App Store policies. The web had become a series of beautiful, but ultimately private, walled gardens.

Web3 emerged not as a new product, but as a new philosophy, a set of foundational principles for building a different kind of internet. If Web1 was read-only and Web2 was read-write, the promise of Web3 was read-write-own. It was a movement predicated on the idea of returning ownership and control to the individual user. It proposed to rebuild the foundational services of the internet—identity, payments, data storage, and computation—on a new and radically different type of infrastructure: one that was not owned by any single company, but by its users collectively. The technological heart of this new movement was the blockchain.

At its core, a blockchain is simply a new kind of database. Unlike a traditional database, which is controlled by a single administrator (like a bank or a SaaS company), a blockchain is a shared, distributed, and immutable ledger. It is a digital record book that is copied and spread across a vast network of computers, known as nodes. When a new transaction occurs, it is broadcast to the network, verified by the participants, and then permanently added to the chain as a new "block." This process, secured by complex cryptography, ensures that once a record is added, it can never be altered or deleted. This creates a single, verifiable source of truth that does not require trusting a central intermediary.

The first and most famous application of this technology was Bitcoin, which used a blockchain to create a decentralized form of digital money. The true catalyst for the Web3 movement, however, was the launch of Ethereum in 2015. Ethereum took the core idea of a distributed ledger and added a crucial, world-changing ingredient: the smart contract. A smart contract is not a legal agreement, but a piece of code. It is a self-executing program that lives on the blockchain, its rules immutably baked into the ledger. These contracts are the backend logic for this new, decentralized web. They allow developers to create complex rules and applications that run exactly as programmed, without the possibility of downtime, censorship, or interference from a central administrator.

This new technological stack gave rise to a new type of application: the decentralized application, or dApp. On the surface, a dApp might look and feel like any other website or mobile app. The revolutionary difference lies in its plumbing. Instead of a frontend that communicates with a private backend running on a company's AWS servers, a dApp's frontend communicates directly with the shared, public backend of a blockchain. The user's identity is not a username and password stored in the company's database, but a cryptographic "wallet," a piece of software like MetaMask that the user controls and which gives them the sole authority to interact with the dApp on their own terms.

This architecture fundamentally changes the user's relationship with the software. In the SaaS world, you are a subscriber. In the dApp world, you are a direct participant. This ownership model was most vividly demonstrated by the explosion of Decentralized Finance, or DeFi. DeFi projects set out to rebuild the entire global financial system from the ground up, replacing traditional, centralized institutions with open protocols running on smart contracts. Platforms like Uniswap created automated, decentralized exchanges where users could trade digital assets directly from their own wallets, without needing a bank or a brokerage as an intermediary. Services like Aave and Compound built decentralized lending markets, where users could lend or borrow assets based on transparent, algorithmically-determined interest rates. The rules were the code, and the code was the law.

The concept of digital ownership was further crystallized by the phenomenon of the Non-Fungible Token, or NFT. While early media attention focused on NFTs as wildly expensive digital art, the underlying technology represented a far more profound innovation: a universal standard for proving ownership of a unique digital item. An NFT is simply a token on a blockchain that points to a specific asset, be it an image, a piece of music, a virtual sword in a video game, or a ticket to a concert. For the first time, digital scarcity was real and verifiable, creating the potential for true economies of digital goods that were not locked inside the walled garden of a single platform.

With this new infrastructure for finance and ownership in place, a new model for corporate governance began to emerge: the Decentralized Autonomous Organization, or DAO. A DAO is an internet-native organization, a kind of digital co-operative, where the rules of operation are encoded in smart contracts and all decisions are made through a voting process by its members, who typically hold the organization's native governance token. DAOs were formed for a dizzying array of purposes, from managing

DeFi protocols and investing in startups to buying rare historical artifacts. They represented a radical experiment in creating organizations that were more transparent, democratic, and less hierarchical than their traditional corporate counterparts.

However, as this new, decentralized world was being built, a deep and revealing paradox began to surface. For all its philosophical commitment to decentralization, the Web3 ecosystem was, in practice, leaning heavily on the very centralized infrastructure it sought to replace. Building and running a full node to directly interact with a blockchain like Ethereum is a technically complex and resource-intensive task. To get around this, most dApps and wallets began to rely on a small handful of specialized service providers that would run the nodes for them and provide access via a simple API.

The most popular of these providers was a service called Infura. For years, Infura acted as the default "on-ramp" to the Ethereum network for a huge swath of the ecosystem. The problem, as many critics pointed out, was that Infura itself was a traditional, centralized cloud company, running its entire operation on the servers of Amazon Web Services. This created a glaring single point of failure. If AWS had an outage, or if Infura for any reason decided to cut off access, a significant portion of the "decentralized" internet would simply stop working. This was not a hypothetical risk; on several occasions, Infura service disruptions caused widespread outages across many popular dApps and wallets, a stark reminder of the movement's lingering dependence on the old guard.

This created an odd symbiosis. The cloud empires, far from seeing Web3 as an existential threat, saw it as a massive new market opportunity. They were not interested in fighting the gold rush; they were perfectly happy to sell the picks and shovels. AWS launched its Amazon Managed Blockchain service. Google Cloud rolled out a suite of tools for node hosting and began using its powerful BigQuery platform to index and analyze blockchain data. Microsoft heavily promoted its Azure Blockchain Service. Their pitch was a pragmatic one: building on the blockchain is hard, so let us manage the complicated and expensive infrastructure for you. The result was a hybrid world, where the core logic of an application might be decentralized on a public blockchain, but the nodes, the frontends, and the data indexing services that made it usable were often hosted on the same centralized cloud platforms as any other SaaS company.

This tension extended to the business model itself. The SaaS world was built on the simple and elegant foundation of the recurring subscription. The Web3 world, by contrast, was powered by a new and often bewildering field of study known as "tokenomics." Most dApp projects are built around a native cryptographic token, which serves as the lifeblood of its internal economy. This token is not just a currency; it can be a multi-purpose tool. It can be a "governance token," giving its holders the right to vote on changes to the protocol. It can be a "utility token," required to access certain features of the service. And it can be an "incentive token," distributed as a reward to early users and liquidity providers to bootstrap the network's growth.

This model created a powerful new dynamic, blurring the lines between user, developer, and investor. An early user of a dApp was not just a customer; by earning or buying the native token, they became a partial owner of the network, with a vested financial interest in its success. This created a potent form of community-driven marketing and a network effect that was baked into the very economic fabric of the protocol. It was a fundamental challenge to the traditional SaaS model, where the value created by the network of users is captured almost exclusively by the company's shareholders. In Web3, the value could, in theory, be distributed more equitably among the participants who created it.

For all its revolutionary potential, however, the Web3 wave repeatedly crashed against the hard shores of reality. The first and most significant challenge was scalability. A blockchain like Ethereum, by design, prioritizes security and decentralization over speed. The result was a network that was slow, capable of processing only a handful of transactions per second, and, during periods of high demand, absurdly expensive to use. A simple transaction could cost a user tens or even hundreds of dollars in "gas fees," the payment required to compensate the network's validators. This made the technology completely impractical for the vast majority of mainstream applications. The industry's response was the development of "Layer 2" scaling solutions, separate blockchains that run on top of the main chain, designed to be faster and cheaper, but this added yet another layer of complexity for users and developers.

The second, and perhaps even greater, hurdle was the user experience. Interacting with the world of dApps in its early stages was a hostile and unforgiving experience for anyone outside a small circle of crypto-natives. Users had to learn to navigate a confusing new world of browser extension wallets, cryptographic addresses, seed phrases, and gas fee management. Sending money to the wrong address or falling victim to a phishing scam could result in an irreversible loss of funds, with no customer support line to call for help. The user-centric, design-led philosophy that had come to define the best of SaaS was almost entirely absent. The tools were powerful, but they were the digital equivalent of the command-line interface, a world away from the simple, one-click elegance that modern consumers had come to expect.

The security landscape was equally treacherous. While the underlying blockchains themselves proved to be remarkably secure, the smart contracts built on top of them were a hacker's paradise. A single flaw in a few lines of code could create a vulnerability that allowed attackers to drain millions of dollars from a protocol in a matter of minutes. The immutable nature of the blockchain meant that these heists were often permanent. The history of DeFi became a litany of spectacular, nine-figure exploits, a constant and brutal reminder of the immense risks of operating on this new frontier.

Finally, the entire ecosystem existed in a state of profound regulatory uncertainty. Governments around the world struggled to understand this new technology and how it fit into existing legal frameworks for securities, banking, and taxation. The lack of clear rules of the road created a chilling effect for many builders and made it difficult for large, conservative enterprise customers to seriously consider adopting the technology.

The Web3 movement, therefore, represents the first truly profound philosophical challenge to the centralized model of the cloud empires. It is not just a new set of technologies, but a competing vision for the future of the internet, one built on a foundation of distributed trust, user ownership, and open, permissionless protocols. It is a vision that is still in its infancy, burdened by immense technical, usability, and regulatory challenges. The question that remains is whether this decentralized wave will ultimately break and recede, leaving behind only a few niche applications, or whether it will mature into a genuine tidal force, one that either erodes the foundations of the existing cloud empires or, perhaps more likely, is channeled and tamed by them, its most potent ideas absorbed into a new, hybrid future for software.

CHAPTER TWENTY-FIVE: The Next Generation of Cloud Empires: Predicting the Future

The story of the cloud, as we have charted it, has been one of relentless abstraction. It began with the abstraction of the physical server, replacing a humming box in a closet with a virtual machine in a distant data center. It progressed to the abstraction of the application itself, transforming a piece of installed software into a service accessed through a browser. The journey continued, abstracting away the operational burden with serverless functions and extending the cloud's reach to the physical world with the edge. Each step has been a move away from the machine and toward the service, away from the implementation and toward the outcome. This journey is far from over. The cloud empires of today, for all their scale and power, have merely built the foundational infrastructure for a world that is about to become far more intelligent, autonomous, and deeply integrated with our physical reality. The end of the beginning is here, and the next generation of empires is already being forged.

The cloud of tomorrow will no longer be a destination, a place where data is sent for processing. It will be an ambient, intelligent fabric woven into the world around us. This is the culmination of the edge computing frontier, a shift from a centralized model to a distributed continuum of computation. The relentless miniaturization of processors and the rollout of high-bandwidth, low-latency networks like 5G are the catalysts for this change. The cloud is escaping the data center and becoming a pervasive, invisible utility. This will give rise to a new and massive category of "physical-world SaaS," platforms designed to manage and automate industries that have, until now, been only lightly touched by the digital revolution.

Imagine a global logistics network managed not from a central command center, but by the network itself. Every shipping container, every pallet, and every delivery vehicle is a smart node on the edge. These nodes communicate with each other, autonomously negotiating routes in real-time to avoid port congestion, rerouting shipments based on weather patterns, and even self-diagnosing mechanical issues before they cause a breakdown. The software that manages this is not a single application, but a distributed intelligence, its decisions being made in milliseconds on a cargo ship in the Pacific or a delivery drone over a city. The cloud becomes the nervous system for the world's physical economy.

Similarly, in agriculture, the cloud will move from the farmer's office to the field itself. A fleet of autonomous tractors and drones, equipped with sophisticated sensors and on-board AI, will manage a farm with microscopic precision. These edge devices will analyze soil moisture on a plant-by-plant basis, identify and remove individual weeds without the need for broad-spectrum herbicides, and apply fertilizer with an efficiency that is impossible for a human operator. The "SaaS" for this new era of farming is a platform that orchestrates this fleet of robotic workers, its code running not just in a data center, but in the intelligent implements that are physically tending the land.

This diffusion of intelligence into the physical world will be mirrored by a similar transformation inside the enterprise. The software that runs our businesses today, for all its AI-powered features, is still fundamentally a tool that requires a human operator. The next generation will be less of a tool and more of a colleague, and eventually, a fully autonomous digital employee. The "copilot" is the friendly, transitional phase. The end state is the autonomous agent. The future enterprise will not just subscribe to a SaaS application; it will hire a team of specialized AI agents to perform entire business functions.

A company's finance department might consist of a handful of human strategists overseeing a team of digital agents. An "Accounts Payable Agent" will ingest all invoices, validate them against contracts, and schedule payments. A "Financial Planning and Analysis Agent" will continuously monitor the business's performance against its budget, generate rolling forecasts, and alert the human executives to emerging risks and opportunities. This will lead to the rise of "headless SaaS," incredibly powerful backend platforms that have no traditional user interface at all. They are managed entirely by AI and communicate with other systems, and their human overseers, through APIs and natural language. The value is not in the clicks, but in the automated outcomes.

This shift toward autonomous, agent-based software will naturally lead to a fundamental re-imagining of the software stack itself. The era of the monolithic, all-in-one SaaS suite that attempts to be everything to everyone is drawing to a close. The new paradigm is the "composable enterprise." Businesses will no longer buy a single, massive platform. Instead, they will assemble their own unique operational fabric from a vast marketplace of smaller, more specialized, and highly interoperable components. These will not just be "microservices" in the technical sense, but "micro-SaaS" in the business sense.

A marketing team, for example, might assemble its "marketing OS" by combining a best-in-class email delivery service from one vendor, a powerful AI-powered copywriting agent from another, a social media scheduling component from a third, and a sophisticated analytics engine from a fourth. These components will be stitched together not by a team of engineers, but by a marketing operations professional using a new generation of intelligent, low-code orchestration platforms. The competitive advantage for a software vendor will shift from having the longest feature list to being the most useful, connectable, and reliable building block in this new, modular ecosystem.

As software is unbundled, so too is the very concept of data ownership. The philosophical challenge posed by the Web3 movement, for all its early struggles with usability and scalability, has planted a powerful and enduring idea: users should own and control their digital identity and data. While the dream of a fully decentralized internet remains distant, the most potent principles of Web3 are beginning to be absorbed into the mainstream, creating a new, hybrid model that blends the convenience of the cloud with the user-centric principles of the blockchain.

The future of logging into a SaaS application may not involve a password or a "Sign in with Google" button. Instead, it will use a decentralized identity system, where a user controls their own digital wallet that holds their verifiable credentials. They grant an application permission to access certain aspects of their identity, and they can revoke that permission at any time. This fundamentally changes the power dynamic, moving from a model where the platform owns the customer relationship to one where the customer owns their own identity and brings it with them across the web.

This concept of digital ownership will extend beyond identity. The next generation of SaaS platforms will use tokenization and NFTs not as speculative assets, but as a practical and powerful tool for community engagement and value distribution. Imagine a collaborative design platform where a user who creates a widely used and highly-rated design template is automatically rewarded with governance tokens in the platform. These tokens not only have a real financial value but also give the user a vote in the future direction of the product. The most valuable contributors are no longer just "power users"; they become genuine stakeholders and co-owners of the network, their incentives perfectly aligned with the success of the platform. This is the pragmatic integration of the ownership economy, a direct challenge to the purely extractive model of Web2.

As these new models take shape, the competitive battlefield for the next generation of cloud empires will shift to a new and decisive terrain: the battle for the AI layer. The ultimate, defensible moat will no longer be the stickiness of the software or the network effect of its users, but the unique intelligence of the proprietary AI models that power the service. The most valuable companies will be those that have amassed a massive, unique dataset and used it to train a "frontier model" that is an order of magnitude more capable than its rivals for a specific industry or function.

The capital investment required to train these foundational models is staggering, running into the hundreds of millions or even billions of dollars. This reality suggests a future of further consolidation, where the existing tech giants, with their vast data centers and deep pockets, become the primary providers of large-scale, general-purpose intelligence. They will be the AI foundries, the TSMCs of the intelligence age. However, a powerful counter-current is emerging from the open-source community. The release of powerful, open-source AI models is democratizing access to this new technology, allowing smaller, more agile startups to fine-tune these models on specialized datasets, creating highly capable, domain-specific intelligence without the need for massive upfront investment. The future will likely be a mix of both: a handful of massive, general-purpose "public utility" AIs from the incumbents, and a vibrant ecosystem of specialized models from a new wave of challengers.

As the software itself becomes more intelligent and ambient, our methods for interacting with it will undergo their most profound change since the invention of the mouse. The flat glass screen will cease to be our primary portal to the digital world. The rise of spatial computing, delivered through increasingly lightweight and powerful augmented and virtual reality headsets, will create a new, immersive interface for enterprise software. An architect and an engineer, located on opposite sides of the world, will be able to walk through a full-scale holographic "digital twin" of a building, making changes and resolving conflicts in real-time. A factory manager will be able to look at a piece of machinery and see a live overlay of its performance data, its maintenance history, and AI-powered diagnostic information. The data of the cloud will be rendered onto the physical world.

This spatial interface will be complemented by a move toward truly conversational interaction. We will simply talk to our software, not as we do with the simple command-and-response voice assistants of today, but in rich, contextual, and collaborative dialogues. The AI will not just be a passive recipient of commands; it will be a proactive participant in the conversation, asking clarifying questions, offering suggestions, and anticipating needs. The user interface will disappear, replaced by a conversation with the intelligence that powers the enterprise.

This increasingly intelligent and interconnected world will not be a single, unified global village. The trend of geopolitical fragmentation, the "splinternet," will solidify. The world will be carved into a handful of distinct digital spheres of influence, each with its own data privacy laws, AI safety regulations, and preferred technology standards. The next generation of cloud empires will not be able to have a single, one-size-fits-all global strategy. They will be forced to become digital chameleons, with modular architectures that allow them to deploy highly localized versions of their platforms that comply with the unique rules of each digital bloc. Navigating the complex and often contradictory demands of this new world order will become a core and critical business function.

The revolution that began with a simple idea—"No Software"— has matured into the invisible infrastructure of the modern world. But its work is far from complete. The future of the cloud is not a simple extrapolation of the past. It is a story of intelligence becoming ambient, of software becoming autonomous, and of the digital and physical worlds fusing into a single, collaborative reality. The empires of the next generation will be defined not by the applications they build, but by the intelligence they harness and the real-world outcomes they automate. The cloud is finally preparing to move beyond the screen and to remake the world in its own image.

www.ingramcontent.com/pod-product-compliance
Lightning Source LLC
LaVergne TN
LVHW051342050326
832903LV00031B/3687